The Evolution of the Future Revisited

Frank W. Elwell

Books by Frank W. Elwell:

Macro Social Theory was previously published as *Macrosociology: The Study of Sociocultural Systems (2009/2015)*

Sociocultural Systems: Principles of Structure and Change (2013)

Macrosociology: Four Modern Theorists (2006)

A Commentary on Malthus' 1798 Essay on Population as Social Theory (2001)

Industrializing America: Understanding Contemporary Society through Classical Sociological Analysis (1999)

The Evolution of the Future Revisited (1991/2015)

4

FOR MY CHILDRENS' CHILDREN

Once the governing human metaphor was pastoral or agricultural, and it clarified, and so preserved in human care, the natural cycles of birth, growth, death, and decay. But modern humanity's governing metaphor is that of the machine. Having placed ourselves in charge of creation, we began to mechanize both the creation itself and our conception of it. We began to see the whole creation merely as raw material, to be transformed by machines into a manufactured paradise.

--Wendell Berry 1977

Table of Contents

Acknowledgments

It is good to have the support of family and friends, and I thank them for the encouragement and conversations. I owe a special note of gratitude to Dr. Dennis Poplin who left behind a critique of the original manuscript that I received too late for the first edition, but which I heeded in this iteration. I continue to appreciate my friends from Murray who gave encouragement for the first edition including Lillian and Charles Daughaday, Ken Carstens, and Mike Miller. At Rogers State University I thank my Administrative Assistant, Shelly Borgstrom, who often keeps me out of trouble, and my good friends David Newcomb and Davis Joyce who constantly challenge me to do better. I thank Patricia who keeps me focused on family. Finally, I need to thank my girls: Melissa, Teresa, Megan and Bree. I dedicated the first edition to them, this second edition is for the grandchildren, born and yet to be.

Preface

The Evolution of the Future (1991) was my first attempt at writing a book. The goal was to write what is called a "trade book," one that would bring sociological insight to the masses and help them form an accurate picture of what is going on out there. Published by Praeger, it suffered many of the flaws of a first real book (dissertations are but warm-ups) by an academic—some academic jargon and an assumption that the reader already had a thorough grounding in the author's discipline. Since that time I have written five more books, I believe I have learned to write clearer prose and deepened my knowledge of "big-picture" sociology with each.

In early 2012 I received notice that Praeger Publishers no longer had *The Evolution of the Future* in print. I asked them for the publishing rights, and they graciously granted them to me. On review of the manuscript I was pleasantly surprised to see that the basic argument had held up so well in the preceding 20 years—something very important if your book is about forecasting the future. I decided to prepare the manuscript as an electronic book and offer it for a modest price online. I changed very little of the manuscript, polishing some of the prose here and there to translate the jargon, adding a line or two for the sake of clarity, or a paragraph or two to better illustrate a point made in the original work; readers will be able to spot these substantive additions by their reference to works or events after 1991.The only change of real substance is this Preface, the Introduction, and a short Addendum at the end of the last chapter.

Heavily influenced by the work of the classical sociologist Max Weber, as well as contemporaries such as Gerhard Lenski and Marvin Harris this book takes a *systems* view of human societies that gives central place to the ways in which society adapts to its environment for needed food, energy, and resources. As environments change through either natural or man-made causes, sociocultural systems must continue to adapt through changes in technology, work patterns, or population level and growth. So central is the adaptation process to human survival that all other widespread components of the sociocultural system—social institutions (such as family, government, economic), and culture (ideas, ideologies, beliefs and values)—must be compatible with the adaptation process. However, the materialist theory that guides these pages is not pushing a simple one-way causal order from material conditions to social structures and cultural superstructures. For we are dealing with a sociocultural *system* and this means that the various parts of that system affect and are affected by other parts as well as by the whole system itself. It is from this systems view that *The Evolution of the Future Revisited* examines and critiques the forecasts of ecologists, technologists, utopians, and dystopians of the recent past and makes a few predictions of its own.

Frank W. Elwell
June 1, 2012

Introduction

Here is the thesis of this book: the future is a function of the past and the present, of history and theory. The simple trend analysis practiced by many futurists is a flawed strategy for forecasting social change. Without knowledge of history, "trendies" assumed that industrial society was some 200 years old and thus ripe for transition to something new; in fact, the first society that could legitimately be called industrial was Great Britain at about the turn of the 20th century, when slightly less than 50 percent of the workforce was engaged in agricultural pursuits. I go further than this and argue that the first real "full-tilt" boogie industrial society did not emerge until America after World War II when the industries of the Arsenal of Democracy were converted to serving consumer society and our family, government, and corporate institutions—as well as our cultural values and beliefs—adapted to this new reality. Many futurists looked at these developments and thought it represented a whole new direction when in fact it was merely the intensification of the industrial mode of production itself.

Worse in terms of their forecasts, many futurists are remarkably ignorant of the physical limits of societies. All sociocultural systems must exploit their environment in order to survive; all must adapt to environmental limits (depletion and pollution) through population and production practices. Industrial society under the direction of capital has a history of intensifying its industrial production that is, extracting more energy and raw materials from the environment as well as fashioning more goods and providing more services through the market economy over time. Adaptation is an ongoing process as both the environment and the technologies change. Many futurists have an extraordinary faith in the ability of technology to continuously overcome environmental limits. They seem to assume that technology will always be developed to address environmental concerns on time and without economic costs or effect on other parts of the system. But this is simply faith—a faith counter to physical laws, the character of sociocultural systems, and human experience.

Futurists who rely almost exclusive on simple trend analysis also completely ignore the existence of elites, positing that new technologies, in-and-of-themselves, will cause the traditional hierarchies of power and authority to crumble. They seem to have missed the long-standing trend of the centralization and enlargement of bureaucracy, instead spotting "trends" of decentralization and individual empowerment. They spot an explosion of service jobs not recognizing that service jobs have grown faster than manufacturing jobs in the United States since the 1870s. They equate "service and information jobs" with professionals and computer programmers when census numbers clearly indicate that the bulk of these jobs are kitchen helpers, nurses' aides and orderlies, and lower level clerks and typists; most of these jobs are of lower prestige and pay than the manufacturing jobs they are replacing. In sum, the trendies posit an unlikely, impossible future unconnected with the past or present.

This book begins by outlining a materialist theory of sociocultural systems, how they are structured and how they change over time. Based on Marvin Harris' theory of cultural materialism, I present a modified version in which I have integrated Weber's theory of bureaucracy and what he called the "rationalization process." Simply put, rationalization is goal oriented rational behavior. In the past, Weber writes, men and women were motivated not only by goal oriented rationality, but also by tradition, emotions, and values derived from spiritual or philosophic concerns. But the modern era, Weber said, places overwhelming emphasis upon the practical, upon goal oriented rationality at the expense of the other three basic motivators. He rooted this change in human behavior to changes in the social structure of modern societies, specifically the growth of bureaucracy. The growth of bureaucracy, in turn, is caused by growth in population and the complexity of production. "The bureaucratic structure goes hand in hand with the concentration of the material means of management in the hands of the master. This concentration occurs, for instance, in a well-known and typical fashion in the development of big capitalist enterprises, which find their essential characteristics in this process. A corresponding process occurs in public organizations" (Weber 1921/1968, 980).

While the first chapter outlines the structure of materialist theory the second chapter details how societies evolve as the result of the intensification-adaptation process. Intensification has led to incredibly complex production systems as well as vast populations. Public and private bureaucracy has grown to provide the coordination and control needed by this intensifying infrastructure. As bureaucracy centralize and enlarge goal oriented rational behavior becomes ever more characteristic in the social order. Rationalization becomes a habit of thought, the way that modern men and women interpret and act upon their world. A good American English translation of the term is *technocratic thinking*. It is the mode of thought that allows corporations to fight against the safety regulations of their products, or dump unsafe products that are banned in the U.S. in developing nations all in the pursuit of profit. It is the same type of thinking that allows those charged with the protection of civil liberties to wiretap, perform illegal searches, and engage in the torture of suspects.

Chapter 3 Oligarchy focuses on the enlargement, centralization, and power of corporate and government bureaucracy in modern American society. This chapter gauges the power of elites that control these bureaucracies, the significant coordination among government and corporate entities, as well as their overriding interest in economic growth. Economic expansion and growth allows elites to maintain their positions without cost to their own wealth, and allows governments to continue in power.

Chapters 4 and 5 deal with the basic conflict within American society between those who believe technology will continue to resolve all environmental problems and those who believe that society must reduce its ecological footprint for long-term sustainability. While both sides use science to buttress their position, the debate is actually beyond science and is rooted in structural interests and cultural values. It is in the interests of those who benefit most from the present system to deny the severity of the ecological crisis and/or to assert that technology can be relied upon to solve these problems as they arise. Those opposed to this view claim that the ecological crisis is indeed severe and that only a massive reorientation of our technology to integrate principles of ecology and a reduction of population will assure the long-term survivability of human society. It is a debate over the future and each side has a very different conception of what sort of future is both attainable *and* desirable.

The interests of corporate and government elites is in continuing business as usual, that is, continue intensify production while ignoring the environmental and social problems such intensification is creating. We are structured for economic growth, and we will continue to try to use technology to overcome any environmental constraints of depletion and pollution that this growth causes. To dissuade the elite from this track will take more than science, it will take a revolution. Based on this it is a safe prediction that industrial societies in general and American society in particular, will continue to intensify production processes, and that world population will continue to grow for the foreseeable future. In accordance with basic materialist theory as well as recent history, this continued intensification will affect the environment, our governmental and corporate structures, as well as cultural ideas and ideologies. The remainder of the book examines the effects that infrastructural intensification—that is growth in population and production—is likely to have for the next hundred years or so on the American sociocultural system.

Chapter 1: A World View

The voluntary actions of men may originate in their opinions, but these opinions will be very differently modified in creatures compounded of a rational faculty and corporal propensities from what they would be in beings wholly intellectual.

--T. Robert Malthus, 1798

An awareness of and interest in the future of man and society is an important part of intellectual life. The study of the future is valuable in that it allows us to see our place in the sweep of history from a unique perspective, a perspective that stresses the continuity of social structures, providing not only insight into our possible futures, but our past and present as well. On a more practical level, the study of the future holds the promise of foresight. Foresight will allow us to change society either to achieve a potential outcome (if we judge the possible future desirable) or to avoid it (if we judge it undesirable). Far from merely satisfying our intellectual curiosity, the study of the future holds the promise of both understanding and guiding sociocultural change.

With a few notable exceptions, studies by futurists have yet to live up to this promise. Even a cursory look at futurist literature today reveals serious contradictions in posited futures. Part of the problem lies in methodology. The trick of many futurists, known also to science fiction writers, is to recognize a trend or the beginning of a trend in the present, work out the full implications of that trend, and then extrapolate a future society built around those implications. The trend may consist of the widespread adoption of a particular technology (the computer, for example), a change in social structure (growth in government), or the spread of an idea (equality). In most cases, the futurist identifies several such trends and builds her vision of future society around them. Thus, we have visions of technological and/or socialist utopias, technological and/or totalitarian dystopias, environmental collapse, social breakdown and anarchy, and something vaguely called a "post-industrial" society. All of these visions are rooted in present day trends; all are put forward as probable (sometimes inevitable) futures.

The problem with simple trend analysis is that it is devoid of both explicit theory and any sense of history. Being without theory, the futurist often overlooks the relationships among various technologies, social structures, and cultural values and ideologies. Society is a sociocultural system. While it may not be so tightly integrated as a biological organism, the various parts of society are interconnected. Without an awareness of these connections—that is, a theory—the futurist often builds a contradictory, impossible future.

A second theoretical insight shared by all of the founders of the discipline and the best practitioners of the craft today, is that material conditions have a profound effect on the rest of the sociocultural system. To explain what is going on out there one should first look to the way a society exploits its environment in order to feed, house, and clothe its people. Important characteristics to look at in understanding any society are its natural environment (geography, climate, plant and animal resources, land fertility), relations to other societies, population characteristics (such as level, growth, age-sex structure), and the technology and labor practices used to exploit that environment.

As the earth is finite, human activity inevitably leads to environmental depletions. To give a simplified example: Suppose a small hunting and gathering society is facing hard times as the hunts have not been successful for several months. Animals that were once plentiful have been severely depleted through over hunting. As they are hemmed in by mountains, sea, and other tribes they have limited mobility. There are several possibilities: (1) they could lower their population levels through limiting their births (celibacy, primitive forms of birth control, body trauma abortion) or increasing their death rates (starvation, infanticide, or killing the weak or elderly). All of these methods involve some physical or psychological costs; (2) they can develop more sophisticated hunting practices or technologies to become more efficient hunters. Such developments, of course, would very much depend on a cultural storehouse of knowledge either through invention or contact with other societies; (3) they could continue to deplete the wild foods available in their environment and collapse as a society; or (4) they could develop a different resource base to replace the loss of game, that is, they could domesticate plants and animals and completely change their way of life. Of these four options, the most widely practiced is the first that is social practices aimed at bringing the human population in line with what nature can provide. The second can only be a temporary solution, as adoption of more efficient techniques will bring in more animal protein, but ultimately will lead to even further depletion of the resource base. The third option, collapse, has happened many times in both prehistoric and even historic societies (see Jared Diamond 2005). Finally, the fourth option, the domestication of plants and animals, is achieved most often through contact with other societies that have already undergone the process; pristine domestication, that is the domestication of plants and animals without learning it through such contact is extremely rare, perhaps happening only six or seven times in human history and, as we will see, requires a rare combination of geography, climate, and plants and animals suitable for domestication.

Because there are psychological and physical costs in controlling population before the invention of effective birth control, societies are susceptible to the lure of innovations that will allow them to take more resources from their environments. Thus, by fits and starts, first depending upon cultural innovation and later upon social contact, societies around the world gradually intensified their infrastructures. They became larger in population, more sophisticated in their exploitive technologies, and ever more specialized in their division of labor. The numbers that Australia can support are very much lower when the continent was peopled by hunters and gatherers than it is when peopled by an industrial society that not only depends on intensive agriculture but world trade to support its population.

A third insight that dominates the sociological worldview is that social structure—groups and organizations—matter. Social organizations are responsible for the allocation of goods and services to individuals. There are two basic forms of social organization: primary and secondary groups. Primary groups rely upon the personal relationships of family and community, loosely organized and based on social bonds of affection and familiarity. Secondary organizations tend to be large and impersonally organized around status and role and are coordinated through bureaucracy. As sociocultural systems throughout the world have grown in population and technology, social organizations within societies have become more complex and formally organized in order to coordinate these activities.

There are two other facts about social structure that you should know. First, it isn't just a one way relationship between material conditions and social structure. While material conditions severely constrain social organization, these organizations interact with these material conditions. For example, the intensification of industrial technologies has caused the growth in size and scope of corporations (there are of course other causal factors of corporate growth, we are indeed talking about a system!); these same corporations have invested heavily in the development of new technologies to more efficiently exploit the environment. Second, social organizations have a profound impact on the beliefs, norms, and values of their members.

Many futurists also lack an appreciation for the overwhelming force of history. They lack the ability to recognize new trends as well as to discriminate between trends of major and minor significance. Without any sort of historical or theoretical discipline, the futurist is free to select trends or in some cases create trends out of singular cases that fit in with his/her personal fantasy or nightmare.

Many have long recognized the possibilities of absurdity in simple trend analysis. In fact, there is even a *Journal of Irreproducible Results* devoted to lampooning such scientific nonsense. Perhaps the most famous article published by the journal was "National Geographic, the Doomsday Machine" in which George Kaub predicted that the accumulation of the more than 6.8 million monthly *National Geographic m*agazines (no one ever throws them away) would soon sink the continent 100 feet and we would all be underwater. Another article projects that beach goers, by going home with sand clinging to their bodies, will remove 80 percent of our coastline within 10 years. Clearly, simple trend analysis is not a reliable predictor. Without reference to theory or history, the trends many futurists isolate operate in a vacuum—the full implications are extrapolated without any posited countervailing forces to limit their development.

In lieu of explicit theory, many futurists are guided by one of two very distinct orientations of pessimism or optimism. An overwhelming sense of pessimism appears to dominate the predictions of futurists with backgrounds in ecology or the social sciences. Their prophecies of doom are based upon projections of industrial society rapidly depleting and polluting its environment or, alternatively, evolving into an inhuman system enslaving man. A sense of optimism pervades the predictions of futurists with backgrounds in the business and science. Their optimism is predicated on the further development of science and technology (particularly biochemistry and computers) which will solve all of our most pressing social problems and eventually liberate man from the "burden" of work. The two perspectives of optimism and pessimism serve much the same purpose as social theory—providing an overall world view that directs the observer's attention to a few "key" trends and issues. They differ from social theory, however, in that optimism and pessimism often rest on unstated assumptions. Being implicit and often unexamined, it is easy for these perspectives to control the selection of trends and data without any rational argument having to be made as to why these trends are isolated and other trends ignored. The optimism or pessimism of the observer forms a *Procrustean Bed,* biasing forecasts to fit either the hopes or fears of the futurist.

Not all futurists lack theoretical or historical foundations. The best have a keen sense of both. Unfortunately, most of these lived in the 19th century. Many early social theorists were futurists. Living in essentially agricultural societies, men like Karl Marx, Max Weber, Alexis de Tocqueville, and Herbert Spencer identified the economic and political trends of their day, worked these trends out to their logical conclusions, and made predictions about the future of industrial society with an astonishing degree of accuracy. The difference between these social scientists and most contemporary futurists is that these early social observers were working from an overall theoretical framework that viewed society as a complex interlocking system that had an evolutionary history. The futures they projected were rooted in knowledge of their past and their present. By narrowly focusing on the future to the exclusion of theory and history, many contemporary futurists have severely limited the scope of their vision. To be accurate in its projections, to correctly perform its task and to fulfill its promise, futurism must be firmly rooted in the past and the present, in history and theory.

The purpose of this chapter is to introduce people to the worldview of sociocultural materialism. Sociocultural materialism is a paradigm (or worldview) that accounts for the origin, maintenance, and change of sociocultural systems. In many ways, it is a throwback to the traditional social theory of the 19th century--it represents an attempt to construct a comprehensive open ended theory of society and its effects on the individual. It is precisely because it makes this attempt that it should be of particular interest to students. Because the paradigm is contemporary, sociocultural materialism has the advantage of building on the perspectives and insights of the past as well as the latest empirical and theoretical research in the social sciences. Because it is comprehensive, it is capable of providing a beginning framework for organizing, evaluating, and integrating the diverse perspectives and insights offered by contemporary social observers. Finally, because the paradigm is open-ended, it is still capable of changing in response to these insights. While sociocultural materialism is a synthesis of a variety of insights of both classical and contemporary social scientists, its basic framework owes much to Marvin Harris. Professor Harris was the cultural anthropologist responsible for the most systematic statement of what he called cultural materialist principles as well as the application of these principles in explaining social life. While the perspective to be developed in this chapter can properly be called a cultural materialist perspective, it differs from the paradigm developed by Harris in that it has been revised to more fully encompass sociological concepts and theory. In making these modifications it is not my intention to slight the work of Harris, but to build upon it. While the revisions do not do great violence to Harris's framework, I believe they extend the scope of the paradigm significantly.

Sociocultural materialism differs from the grand theory of the past in that it is both easily comprehensible and lends itself readily to empirical investigation. A systems theory, it incorporates many of the themes of futurist literature (environmental depletion/pollution, technological development, the increasing dominance of rational-scientific thought) in a coherent framework that summarizes the complex web of interrelationships that make up societies. As a paradigm, it offers a multi-causal view of social evolution.

Sociocultural Materialism

Sociocultural materialism begins with the assumption that the various parts of society are interrelated to one another. An institution such as the family cannot be viewed in isolation from the economic, political, or religious institutions of a society. When one part of the society changes it has an effect on other parts of the system. Materialists further assert that the entire structure of the sociocultural system rests on the way a society exploits its environment to meet the biological and psychological needs of its population.

Mankind is relatively free from biological instincts, drives, and predispositions. Rather than relying on instinctual behavior, the vast repertoire of our social behavior is learned. However, there are several biological and psychological constants or universal needs of human beings. In stating these needs, Harris is attempting to list the minimal number of bio-psychological constants needed to account for the similarities as well as the differences in sociocultural evolution. While the needs are universal, the ways in which societies meet these needs and the extent to which these needs are met are highly variable. Harris enumerates four bio-psychological constants:

1. People need to eat and will generally opt for diets that offer more rather than fewer calories and proteins and other nutrients.

2. People cannot be totally inactive, but when confronted with a given task, they prefer to carry it out by expending less rather than more (human) energy.

3. People are highly sexed and generally find reinforcing pleasure from sexual intercourse--more often from heterosexual intercourse.

4. People need love and affection in order to feel secure and happy, and, other things being equal, they will act to increase the love and affection others give them (Harris 1979, 63).

Harris justifies his list with two observations. First, humans share these bio-psychological needs with other primates; thus, its generality is virtually assured. Second, the list should be judged not on its inclusiveness but upon the adequacies of the theories it helps to generate. The more parsimonious the list of constants (or assumptions), the more powerful the theories based upon them.

The Universal Structure of Sociocultural Systems

Like all living organisms, humans must obtain energy from their environment. The need to draw energy out of the environment in order to satisfy the biological and psychological needs of its people is the central task of any society. Therefore, each society must ultimately exist within the constraints imposed by its environment. Chief among these constraints is the availability of natural resources such as energy, land, minerals, and other raw materials. A further constraining factor, only recently recognized by our political-economic systems, is the amount of pollution created by society. While human action can modify these constraints, they cannot be escaped. Human reason tells us that the earth is finite; there is only so much recoverable oil, coal, or other fossil fuels in the ground. Other resources such as iron ore, bauxite, copper, zinc also have limits. Even renewable resources such as food, wood and water have natural limits on the amount that can be, grown, extracted or recycled on an annual basis. In addition to limits of the availability of resources there are also unknown limits on the amount of pollution that can be tolerated by earth's natural systems or by the human beings themselves.

The principal interface between a sociocultural system and its environment is termed the "infrastructure." A society's infrastructure consists of the principle mechanism by which it modifies the type and amount of the resources it needs from its environment in order to sustain its population. The infrastructure is divided into

31

two parts: (1) the mode of production, consisting of technology and work patterns aimed at extracting energy, raw materials, and food from the environment to satisfy its population; and (2) the mode of reproduction consisting of behaviors and technologies aimed at controlling destructive increases or decreases in population size. The modes of production and reproduction are attempts to strike a balance between reproduction and the consumption of energy from a finite environment. These activities are absolutely essential for the survival of any sociocultural system, for the sustainability of life itself; it is for this reason that the infrastructure is considered the foundation upon which the remaining parts of the social system are based.

The structural components of sociocultural systems arise from the necessity of maintaining secure, predictable, and orderly relationships between individuals. The threat of disorder arises primarily from the allocation of labor and the distribution of goods and services to individuals and groups. Social organization (or structure) regulates the allocation and distribution process. Modifying Harris's concept somewhat, the structure can be divided along primary and secondary lines: (1) primary groups, consisting of small groups like the family, that regulate production, reproduction, exchange and consumption within domestic settings; and (2) secondary organizations, or the impersonal organizations such as government and corporations which regulate production, reproduction, exchange, and consumption within and between groups and sociocultural systems. The primary-secondary group dichotomy encompasses *all* human organizations responsible for the allocation and distribution of *all* bio-psychological need satisfaction.

The last component of the sociocultural system is termed the superstructure. The behavioral superstructure includes recreational activities, sports, art, and other aesthetic activities. The behavioral superstructure arises from the importance of leisure activities for the human psyche. The cultural superstructure, on the other hand, is far more important in our considerations of system dynamics and evolution. The cultural superstructure consists of the shared symbols, ideas, ideologies, rules, values, goals, aesthetics, philosophies, science, and knowledge base that guide human behavior. Max Weber identified four basic cultural motivations behind all human action: (1) zweckrational, or rational action in relation to a goal; (2) wertrational, or rational action in relation to a value; (3) affective or emotional action; and (4) traditional action which is dictated by custom or habit. Weber's intended these four basic motivators to be a comprehensive list of the types of meaning men and women give to their conduct across sociocultural systems.

System Dynamics

The major principle of sociocultural materialism is that the modes of production and reproduction determine the primary and secondary group structure, which in turn determines the behavioral and mental superstructure. When trying to understand or explain a widespread social practice or belief, Marvin Harris urges, always begin with an examination of infrastructural-environmental relations. He originally called this the *principle of infrastructural determinism* (a somewhat unfortunate choice of terminology since Harris explicitly recognizes the probabilistic nature of the relationships). Because of misunderstandings and misinterpretations, Harris later renames this principle the *primacy of the infrastructure*. The rationale behind giving the infrastructure such priority rests upon the fact that it is through infrastructural practices that society adapts to its environment. The infrastructure of social systems encompasses the principle sociocultural practices aimed at modifying ecological constraints. It is through infrastructural practices that society modifies the amount and type of resources it requires. Since these infrastructural practices are essential for human life itself, all widespread structural and superstructural practices must be compatible with these practices. Any widespread change in structure and superstructure must be compatible with the existing modes of production and reproduction.

However, while the infrastructure is considered to be of primary importance, the structure and superstructure are not mere reflections of infrastructural processes, but are in interaction with these processes. Materialists view society as a very stable system. The most likely outcome of any change in the system—whether this change begins in the infrastructure, structure, or superstructure—is resistance in the other sectors of the system. This "system maintaining negative feedback" is capable of "deflecting," "dampening," or extinguishing most system change. The result is either the extinction of the innovation or slight compensatory changes that preserve the fundamental character of the whole system. An example of a structural change that received a lot of negative feedback was the commune movement of the 1960s. At the time, many social scientists were predicting that the commune represented a real alternative lifestyle. There were predictions that in the future, we would all have to struggle with the choice of either starting a traditional family or joining a commune. But the commune met harsh resistance (and sanctions) from existing institutions (family, church, local governments), ideologies, and traditions (monogamy, Christianity). In addition, like the extended family before it, the commune does not allow for easy geographic or social mobility of its members. As a result, few of our young are struggling with the choice today.

Not every change that meets resistance in the structure and/or the superstructure is extinguished. Women working outside the home, a change caused by the rising cost of living and a declining birth rate (both infrastructural causes), encountered fierce resistance from the traditional family, many secondary organizations (corporations, unions, churches, government), and from the superstructure (Christianity, sexist ideology, traditions, and beliefs). Despite this opposition, American society is presently adjusting its institutions and ideologies to accommodate the change.

Materialists assert that infrastructural-environmental relationships are central in explaining sociocultural change. But we also recognize the importance of structure and superstructure in determining the speed, character and direction of change. In general, sociocultural change that releases more energy from the environment is likely to be swiftly adapted. But cultural materialism does not rely on the simple calculation of the greatest good for the greatest number of people to account for cultural change. Many changes are more satisfying to some members of society than to others. The biological and psychological well-being of those on top of the sex, age, class, race, caste, or ethnic hierarchies of society will weigh more heavily than the well-being of those at the bottom. Infrastructural changes that enhance the position of these elites are likely to be "amplified and propagated" throughout the entire sociocultural system. Infrastructural changes that undermine these positions will be resisted. The elite of these hierarchies are able to impose direct economic and political sanctions to buttress their position. In addition, they are able to mobilize superstructural support by indirectly encouraging ideas and ideologies favorable to their interests. Cultural materialism is in fundamental agreement with Marx when he states: "The ideas of the ruling class in each epoch are the ruling ideas." This is not to say that economic or political elites always rule in the manner of divine-right kings. The amount of power and control exercised by elites varies across societies and through time. However, there exists within every society a dominant class (or classes) that possesses a disproportionate amount of social power. A cultural materialist analysis attempts to identify this class, gauge the amount of power it wields, and uncover its biases and assumptions when analyzing social systems.

Table 1

Revised Components of Sociocultural Systems

Environment

The physical, biological and chemical constraints to which human action is subject.

Infrastructure

1. Mode of production: The technology and the practices employed for expanding or limiting basic subsistence production, especially the production of food and other forms of energy.

    A. Technology of subsistence.

    B. Techno-environmental relationships.

    C. Division of Labor

2. Mode of reproduction: The technology and the practices employed for expanding, limiting, and maintaining population size.

    A. Demography.

    B. Mating patterns.

    C. Fertility, natality, mortality.

    D. Nurturance of infants.

    E. Medical control of demographic patterns.

    F. Contraception, abortion, infanticide.

Structure

3. Primary group structure: Consists of a small number of people who interact on an intimate basis. They perform many functions, such as regulating reproduction, basic production, socialization, education, and enforcing domestic discipline. Examples:

    A. Family.

    B. Community.

    C. Voluntary organization.

D. Friendship networks.

4. Secondary group structure: These groups may be large or small, but their members tend to interact without any emotional commitment to one another. These organizations are coordinated through bureaucracies. They perform many functions such as regulating production, reproduction, socialization, education, and enforcing social discipline. Examples:

A. Governments, parties, factions, military, and police.

B. Corporations, businesses, and industries.

C. Education, media, and other formal socialization agents.

D. Service and welfare organizations.

E. Professional and labor organizations

Hierarchies based on class, sex, race, caste, age, ethnic, and other statuses exist throughout the structure of society.

Superstructure

5. Behavioral superstructure.

A. Art, music, dance, literature, advertising.

B. Rituals.

C. Sports, games, hobbies.

D. Science.

6. Cultural superstructure: Refers to conscious and unconscious motives for human behavior.

A. Values.

B. Emotions.

C. Traditions.

D. Zweckrational (goal oriented rational action).

*Adapted from Marvin Harris 1979, *Cultural Materialism*, 46-7

Chapter 2: Social Evolution

People are trapped in history and history is trapped in them.

--James A. Baldwin

Theories of social evolution are almost as old as social thought. The ancient Greeks, for example, thought that societies passed through stages. Beginning with a "Golden Age," each succeeding age (Silver, Brass, Heroic, and Iron) was seen as harsher, more degraded than the past one. Throughout history most viewed sociocultural change as leading man away from the ideal social order of antiquity. Such a world view led many to consider their era as cruel and harsh, the future worse still. It wasn't until the end of the seventeenth century that the modern idea of progress was born. Early sociologists were profoundly influenced by this idea of progress, linking their analysis of fundamental structural change under the assault of industrialism to theories about the direction of those changes and their ultimate end point. Spencer, whose evolutionary theories strongly influenced Darwin, used the terms evolution and progress almost interchangeably. For many social thinkers in the early nineteenth century, social evolution was linked to the ultimate triumph of some principle or condition such as equality, material wealth, freedom, or reason.

The close identification of progress and social evolution has led to evolution's decline in modern social thought. Beginning perhaps with Max Weber, sociologists first became disenchanted with the idea of progress and then hostile towards seemingly "unilinear" theories that posited social change in all societies in a common direction. Social evolution fell out of fashion, until recently totally ignored by modern day sociologists.

Intensification

Although it rejects the value-laden notion of progress, sociocultural materialism is an avowedly evolutionary perspective. Throughout history, both productive and reproductive forces have expanded. "Anthropologists have long recognized that in broadest perspective cultural evolution has had three main characteristics: escalating energy budgets, increased productivity and accelerating population growth" (Harris 1979, 67). The reason for the linkage of productivity and population growth lies with the bio-psychological costs of regulating population: Before the development of the state, infanticide, body- trauma abortion, and other malign forms of population control predisposed cultures which were in other respects adjusted to their habitats to increase production in order to reduce the wastage of infants, girls, and mothers. In other words, because prehistoric cultures kept their numbers in line with what they could afford by killing or neglecting their own children, they were vulnerable to the lure of innovations that seemed likely to allow more children to live (Harris 1979, 68-69).

It is this intensification of production and reproduction that provides the driving force behind cultural evolution. Great transitions in human societies—transitions that involve a qualitative shift in the mode of production, say from hunting and gathering to one based on horticulture—

are an outgrowth of the intensification process. Materialists assert that the intensification of existing modes of production and reproduction inevitably leads to environmental depletion, resulting in either the sudden collapse of the cultural system (Easter Island, for example) or a shift to a new mode of production. If a culture successfully shifts to a new mode of production, the intensification process begins again.

By relying upon demographic, technological, and environmental factors, cultural materialists are able to account for such social phenomena as the rise of agriculture, the variety of agricultural societies, the emergence of inequality and the state, the variety of state systems, and the emergence of capitalism in Western Europe. For example, Harris attempts to explain why so many of the world's people chose agriculture as a strategy over hunting and gathering between 10,000 and 2,000 B.C. Relying heavily on the work of Mark Cohen (1977), Harris asserts that because of a change in the natural environment (specifically, the onset of the interglacial period about 13,000 years ago) the labor costs of the hunter-gatherer mode of production rose as the benefits fell. Many prey species became depleted or extinct. "In all centers of early agricultural activity, the end of the Pleistocene saw a notable broadening of the subsistence base to include more small mammals, reptiles, birds, mollusks and insects. Such 'broad spectrum' systems were a symptom of hard times" (Harris 1979, 87). The transition, then, was out of necessity, not the result of accumulated knowledge or the appearance of a genius with an "idea." Indeed, the evidence suggests that hunter-gatherers knew about the relationship between seed and plant. However, knowledge of this relationship did not result in agricultural development until the existing mode of production could no longer meet the bio-psychological needs of the population. Throughout history, the intensification of the forces of production have always been toward greater complexity because the process leads to the exploitation of less available, harder-to-reach sources of energy. Similarly, when environmental depletion is reached, the qualitative shift in the forces of production represents a move from a readily available source of energy (say wood) to a less accessible source (coal, oil, or nuclear fission). Over the course of social evolution, mankind has had to engage in more and more complicated processing and production techniques in order to draw energy out of the environment. In turn, the intensification of the infrastructure leads to the growth of secondary organizations at the expense of primary groups, a process known as bureaucratization.

Bureaucratization of Structure

According to Weber, characteristics associated with bureaucracy include a highly specialized division of labor, a hierarchy of authority, written rules of conduct and authority, impersonality in both employment and in dealing with those outside the organization, advancement within the organization based on expertise, and efficiency. The process of bureaucratization refers to the changes within organizations toward greater rationality, that is, improved operating efficiency and more effective attainment of common goals. Bureaucratization pervades nearly all aspects of modern life including government (all levels), corporations, education, sports, and even crime.

There are five characteristics of the sociocultural system that promote the growth of bureaucracy. Two of these characteristics are of the infrastructure: industrialism and population growth. Two are structural characteristics: the decline of primary groups and the "organizational imperative." And finally, one is a superstructural characteristic: the rationalization process. One of the fundamental reasons behind the emergence and growth of bureaucracies is that they enable large scale tasks to be performed. The use of energy sources other than human and animal power, the growth of mass production, and the increase in job specialization has led to greater needs for coordination of these diverse activities. A modern automobile manufacturing corporation, for example, must coordinate the activities of thousands of employees, suppliers, and dealers around the globe. More complex technologies and markets require rational social organization for coordination, control, and regulation of these activities.

The growth of population has a similar impact on the bureaucratization process. Greater numbers of people require rational social organization for the coordination and regulation of their activities. The world has experienced exponential growth in population over the last two centuries. Thus, it has been necessary to control and supervise large masses of people in an effort to deal more efficiently with their needs and problems (as well as to provide increasing numbers of people with employment opportunities). Bureaucracies meet these kinds of demands. As population has increased, formal organizations have developed to solve problems of adapting to the environment (government and corporations), handling survival needs (sanitation and food production), and providing social services (welfare and medical care).

A third factor behind the growth of bureaucracies is the decline in the size, influence, and importance of primary group organization. Industrial society requires an extremely mobile population. Because of the specialized division of labor, people are required to move from one end of the country to the other in order to engage in their occupations. In addition, the specialized division of labor requires diverse educational and training organizations—it would not do to have our brain surgeons trained at their fathers' knees. Finally, bureaucratic-industrial society requires social mobility as well. This has had the effect of weakening many traditional groups such as the family and the community. In a more traditional society, these groups provide many services to the individual—child care, social security, financial aid, education, social control, medical care, counseling, and a wealth of other services. With the decline of primary groups, many secondary organizations have arisen in industrial society to provide services that used to be performed by these groups.

The rise of bureaucracy, then, is in large part an effort to deal with the breakdown of traditional ways of organizing social life. What the family, community, ethnic groups, friendship network, and church once did private corporations and government now attempt to do. While traditional institutions provided aid and services on the basis of group ties, bureaucracies provide aid and services through contractual legal relationships. While many conservatives argue that it is the expansion of bureaucratic power itself that weakens primary groups, such an argument confuses cause and effect. The traditional ways broke down because of infrastructural intensification—we cannot solve our problems simply by willing families and communities back into existence.

Another structural characteristic that promotes the growth of bureaucracy I call the "organizational imperative." The creation of bureaucracies themselves has often required the creation of other bureaucracies to supervise, control, or deal with them. Government bureaucracies often mediate the struggles between companies or regulate their behavior so that they cannot exploit the powerless or the environment. In the name of education, welfare, taxation, safety, health, and the environment, state bureaucratic power has grown to protect individuals and groups from being exploited by corporations and other secondary organizations. Unions are another example of a bureaucratic organization that arose to give voice to individual workers who were dealing with large scale organizations. Many groups have organized to deal on a more equal basis with already established state and corporate bureaucracies.

Finally, the rationalization process has also promoted the growth of bureaucracies. Bureaucracies are built on the principles of efficiency and calculability. The rationalization process refers to a set of norms and values that increasingly dominate industrial society. It is a habit of thought involving a persistent questioning of the adequacy of means to ends and a constant search for more adequate means. The result is a society that is constantly questioning traditional ways, devising more rational ways to achieve desired ends. Rationalization is the integrating mechanism of modern social life, replacing more traditional institutions and values that are in increasing conflict with the intensifying infrastructure. The rationalization of superstructure provides positive feedback for the further bureaucratization of structure, both of which provide positive feedback for the further intensification of infrastructure.

Rationalization of Superstructure

The rationalization process is the practical application of knowledge to achieve a desired end. It is a social extension of the industrial mode of production itself. "It might be defined as the organization of life through a division and coordination of activities on the basis of an exact study of men's relations with each other, with their tools and their environment, for the purpose of achieving greater efficiency and productivity. Hence it is purely a practical development brought about by man's technological genius" (Freund 1969, 18).

The rationalization of social life has many ramifications. It leads to efficiency, coordination, and control over both the physical and social environment. It is the guiding principle behind bureaucracy, specialization, and the increasing division of labor. Rationalization has led to the unprecedented increase in both the production and distribution of goods and services. It is also associated with secularization, depersonalization, and oppressive routine.

Max Weber viewed rationalization as a tendency that predated industrial development. Rooted in features of Protestant Christianity, Weber identified rationalization as one of the components of the "Spirit of Capitalism" and thus as one of the causes of the industrial revolution. Although many view Weber's formulation of rationalization as a rebuke to Marxian materialism because it supposedly asserts the primacy of an idea in affecting social change, it is not inconsistent with interpretations of Marx made by contemporary scholars (c.f. Harrington 1976). Nor is Weber's formulation of rationalization inconsistent with materialism, which explicitly recognizes the importance of structural interests, ideologies, and ideas in providing feedback to infrastructural development. For example, Harris (1977, 251-267) argues that science and scientific techniques were important superstructural influences in the development of capitalism and industrialism. While materialists assert that environmental-infrastructural relationships are central in explaining why societies must shift to a different mode of production, structures and superstructures play a vital role in determining the character of subsequent change. Weber's analysis of the origins of capitalism is quite consistent with materialist explanations as long as one does not interpret Weber as claiming that such ideal factors can completely account for the transition. And Weber explicitly rejects such an interpretation: "But it is, of course, not my aim to substitute for a one-sided materialistic with an equally one sided spiritualistic causal interpretation of culture and of history. Each is equally possible, but each, if it does not serve as the preparation, but as the conclusion of an

47

investigation, accomplishes equally little in the interest of historical truth" (1904/1930, 183). What Weber is saying here is that many sociocultural factors play a role in social evolution.

The rationalization process is the most general element of Max Weber's sociology. Having helped give birth to industrialization, it (rationalization) became fused with it and was later carried by it. To become industrialized was to become rationalized, a process affecting every area of society, the most public and the most private, the state and the economy as well as the relations of marriage, family and personal friendship (Kumar 1978, 102). As the industrial mode of production intensifies, the rationalization of social and personal life continues apace. Increasingly, human behavior is guided by observation, experiment, and reason to master the natural and social environment to achieve a desired end.

There is a psychic price that we pay as we play our specialized roles and conform to the highly restricting norms of bureaucratic life. Alienation refers to the sense of powerlessness, isolation, and meaninglessness experienced by human beings when they are confronted with social institutions and conditions that they cannot control and consider oppressive. The concept of alienation was introduced to sociology by Karl Marx. In his view, alienation occurs when people lose the recognition that society and social institutions are constructed by human beings and can therefore be changed by them. The social world thus confronts people as uncontrollable, hostile, leaving them alien in the very environment that they have created.

Marx applied this idea to many social institutions such as law, government, religion, and the economy. In the economic order, for example, people establish economic systems, feel powerless to change these systems when they become oppressed by them, and thus become victims of their own institutions. Marx felt the economic order the most important, for he believed that the capacity for labor is one of the most distinctive human characteristics. All other species, he argued, are objects in the world; human beings alone are subjects because they consciously act on and create the world, shaping their lives, cultures, and personalities in the process.

In modern bureaucratic-industrial societies people have become alienated from their work and thus from nature, from other human beings, and from themselves. An important source of alienation is the extreme division of labor in modern industrial societies. Each worker has a specific, restricted, and limited role that makes it impossible to apply the full human capacities of the hands, the mind, and the emotions to work. The worker (or bureaucrat) has diminished responsibility, does not own the tools with which the work is to be done, does not own the final product, does not set the organizational goals, does not set the hours or the pace, does not have the right to make decisions, and is therefore reduced to a minor part of a process, a mere cog in a machine.

Work then becomes an enforced activity, not a creative or satisfying one. It becomes the means for maintaining existence. It is no longer an expression of the man himself; it is a means to an end. While alienation is most evident in the blue-collar jobs in which the work is so routine and boring that the worker takes only a minimum of interest in what he is doing, it is becoming increasingly common in highly specialized white-collar and professional jobs as well.

General Rationalization

Weber's general theory of rationalization (of which bureaucratization is but a particular case) refers to increasing human mastery over the natural and social environment. The essential tools for this mastery are those of observation, experiment, and reason. The "intensification of the infrastructure" can be interpreted as the growing application of goal oriented rational behavior (technology being the obvious example) to regulate the flow of energy from the environment—and thus another form of the rationalization process itself. While the rationalization of the infrastructure throughout most of human history led to the growth of population, both to satisfy the structural interests of hierarchies and the biological and psychological needs of the people, an advanced industrial society has somewhat different interests and emphasizes other needs. Rapid population growth in advanced industrial societies has obviously stopped, but the sociocultural practices used to achieve this stability, as well as the changing feedback loops of structure and superstructure, are clearly consistent with rationalization (cf. Harris 1981, 76-97). A similar case can be made with respect to the mode of production. The distinguishing characteristic of the changing mode of production is not one of growth but of rationalization, or the increasing application of science and reason to the problems of drawing energy out of the environment. This rationalization of infrastructure is caused by the continued depletion/pollution of the natural environment.

The intensification of the infrastructure is paralleled by the increasing application of the method and substance of science in the structure and superstructure: more complex technologies and greater numbers of people require rational social organization for coordination and control. The intensification of the infrastructure leads to the growth of secondary organizations at the expense of primary groups. In turn, these changes in social structure have changed human character through changing values, philosophies, and beliefs in the superstructure of society. Such superstructural norms and values as individualism, efficiency, self-discipline, materialism, and calculability (all of which are part of Weber's concept of zweckrational) have been encouraged by the bureaucratization process. Finally, it should be emphasized that the relationships between the various components of the system are dynamic. The rationalization of superstructure provides positive feedback for the further bureaucratization of structure, both of which provide positive feedback for the further intensification of infrastructure.

The Irrationality of Rationalization

As bureaucracies satisfy and satiate us with their output of goods and services, they also shape our mentality. Ultimately, rationalization involves dehumanization—the elimination of concern for human values. The assembly line is designed to eliminate human variability; the technology often operates in ways that are contrary to human needs and values. The rationalization process, as indicated previously, is the increasing dominance of zweckrational over rational action based on values, or actions motivated by traditions and emotions. Zweckrational can best be understood as "technocratic thinking," in which the goal is simply to find the most efficient means to whatever ends are defined as important by those in power.

An extreme case of rationalization was the extermination camps of Nazi Germany. The goal was to kill as many people as possible in the most efficient manner, and the result was the ultimate of dehumanization—the murdering of millions of men, women, and children. The men and women who ran the extermination camps were, in large part, ordinary human beings. They were not particularly evil people. Most went to church on Sundays; most had children, loved animals and life. The cyanide used in the gas chambers was supplied by an old established German firm through competitive bid. Their product could do the most effective job for the least possible cost; so they got the contract. In sum, the extermination camps were models of bureaucratic efficiency using the most efficient means available at that time to accomplish the goals of the Nazi government.

Technocratic thinking (zweckrational) can be contrasted with goal oriented rational behavior which involves the assessment of means in terms of ultimate human values such as social justice, peace, and human happiness. Even though a bureaucracy is highly rational in the formal sense of technical efficiency, it does not follow that it is also rational in the sense of the moral acceptability of its goals or the means used to achieve them. The fact that individual officials have specialized and limited responsibility and authority within the organization means that they are unlikely to raise basic questions regarding the moral implications of the overall operations of the organization. In an advanced industrial society everything becomes a component of the expanding machine, including human beings.

Specialization has been called the disease of modern man. Under the rule of specialization, society becomes more and more intricate and interdependent, but with less common purpose. The community disintegrates because it loses its common bond. The emphasis in bureaucracies is on getting the job done in the most efficient manner possible. Consideration of what impact organizational behavior might have on society as a whole, on the environment, or the consumer simply does not enter into the calculation.

The problem is further compounded by the decline of many traditional institutions such as the family, community, and religion which served to bind pre-industrial man to the interests of the group. Rationalization implies the weakening of traditional and religious moral authority (secularization); the values of efficiency and achievement predominate. The result is a seeming paradox—bureaucracies, the epitome of rationalization, acting in very irrational ways. Thus we have economic bureaucracies in pursuit of profit which deplete and pollute the environment upon which they are based; political bureaucracies set up to protect our civil liberties, violate them with impunity. This can be called the irrationality of rationalization, or more specifically, the irrationality of zweckrational.

Wendell Berry, the Kentucky poet and conservationist, fully illustrates the theory of sociocultural materialism in his book *The Unsettling of America* (1977). While Berry's inquiry into the changes occurring in American agriculture is deeply personal and often poetic, his analysis and insights are remarkably consistent with the theory. While his focus is on agriculture, Berry believes that the industrialization of the American farm is but a part of the larger industrialization process, a process that has similar effects within other sectors of the mode of production.

Like all materialists, Berry's world view begins with man's relationship to the earth. The industrialization of American agriculture has dramatically increased the productivity of the land but at the expense of depleting topsoil, water, and other natural resources. In order to increase production, farmers have relied on mechanization, chemical fertilizers, herbicides, fungicides, and pesticides—all of which pollute the environment and poison the soil. "The so-called 'green revolution' is an oil revolution in which higher crop yields per acre have been made possible by continuous injections of fossil fuel energy into the production of plant varieties specially bred for their ability to respond to petrochemical inputs" (Harris 1977, 284).

Traditional agriculture used about 1 calorie of energy (usually in the form of human or animal labor) to produce 10 calories of food. As David Pimentel of Cornell University has shown, in the United States 2,790 calories of energy are now being used to produce and deliver one can of corn containing 270 calories. The production of beef now requires even more prodigious energy deficits:

22,000 calories to produce 100 grams (containing the same 270 calories as in the can of corn) (Harris 1977: 284). Berry calls this type of agriculture exploitive, an extractive industry in which maintenance and care for the land has given way to short-term production goals. Based on huge capital outlays this type of agriculture promotes the growing concentration of farmland in order to achieve economies of scale. Based on non-renewable resources, this type of agriculture is sustainable only so long as supplies of oil remain plentiful.

Concurrent with the industrialization of agriculture is the decline of farm families and communities. Each year farm holdings have become larger, owners fewer. Berry contrasts the industrialization of American farms with forced collectivization in the Soviet Union: "I remember, during the fifties, the outrage with which our political leaders spoke of the forced removal of the populations of villages in communist countries. I also remember that at the same time, in Washington, the word of farming was 'Get big or get out'—a policy which is still in effect and which has taken an enormous toll. The only difference is that of method; the force used by the communists was military; with us, it has been economic—a 'free market' in which the freest were the richest" (Berry 1977, 41).

The people moved off the land often gravitate to large urban areas, many to become a permanent underclass, excluded from participation in modern society. Industrial farming has not only destroyed farming communities, but has contributed to the disintegration of urban life. Berry points out that between 1960 and 1974 the number of American farms has decreased by 25%, while larger units (more than $20,000 a year in sales) went up by 80%. Further, in 1971 only about 20% of the largest farms received about 80% of all farm income. The centralization of American agriculture has continued to the present day. "In the U.S., the total number of farms has fallen from an all-time high of over 6.3 million to just over 2.2 million. Meanwhile, the average size per farm nearly tripled between 1900 and 2007, from 147 to 418 acres...Small-scale family farms (defined as operator-owned farms with less than $250,000 in sales — which does *not* mean $250,000 in profit, of course) make up 88.3% of all farms in the U.S., while large-scale family farms (operator-owned farms with sales over $250,000) are 9.3%...Large scale family farms account for 66 percent of production" (Sharp 2011).

Berry convincingly demonstrates that the intensification of American agriculture has been promoted by a collaboration of *agribusinessmen* within corporations, *agriscientists* within the university, and bureaucrats within government agricultural agencies. It is their interests, their ambitions and goals that have determined the direction of agricultural development. As such, it has been the interests of merchants and industrialists, academic careerists and bureaucrats that have guided the industrialization of the farm, "who have promoted so-called efficiency at the expense of community (and real efficiency), and quantity at the expense of quality" (Berry 1977, 42).

What Berry is condemning in modern agricultural bureaucracies is their obsessive focus on the narrow goal of productivity to the exclusion of all other values (zweckrational). "Modern American agriculture has made itself a 'science' and has preserved itself within its grandiose and destructive assumptions by cutting itself off from the moral tradition (as it has done also from the agricultural tradition) and confining its vision and its thought within the bounds of internal accounting" (Berry 1977, 172).

Like the goal oriented behavior of other bureaucracies, the bureaucracies of agriculture ignore tradition and wider social values (care of the land and people) in their attempts to achieve their goal. Of the three bureaucracies promoting the intensification of agriculture, Berry heaps the most scorn upon agricultural professors: "The careerist professor is by definition a specialist professor. Utterly dependent upon his institution, he blunts his critical intelligence and blurs his language so as to exist 'harmoniously' within it—and so serves his school with an emasculated and fragmentary intelligence, deferring 'realistically' to the redundant procedures and meaningless demands of an inflated administrative bureaucracy whose educational purpose is written on its paychecks" (Berry 1977, 148).

The professors, according to Berry, define agriculture in purely commercial terms. Their goal is to promote an agricultural system that provides food as efficiently as possible (meaning quickly, cheaply, with minimum human labor) as well as to provide a market for agricultural machines and chemicals. To advance in academe (or to make one's self marketable for lucrative jobs in the other agricultural bureaucracies), Berry contends, one's research must be oriented toward agribusiness, not the land or the farmers who work it.

The reason that Berry is so hostile to the academician (aside from the fact that he was a professor at the University of Kentucky and knows them well) is because the land grant college system was specifically instituted to promote the interests of the independent farmer (whom Jefferson believed to be the backbone of democracy). Like experts in many bureaucracies, the academics defined their goals in quantitative, measurable terms. Productivity became the yardstick; values concerning the land, the welfare of the farming people themselves, even of the total society were simply not considered. Partly as a result of their research, millions of farmers and farm workers have been forced from the land; the land itself is rapidly becoming depleted and polluted. Consequently, bureaucracies originally set up to help farmers and farm communities actually pursue goals that end up destroying the very groups they are supposed to serve.

Berry describes the general process of the irrationality of rationalization in words that strongly echo Weber: "The practical, divorced from the disciplines of value, tends to be defined by the immediate interests of the practitioner, and so becomes destructive of value, practical and otherwise" (Berry 1977, 158). Berry also perceives the corrosive effects of excessive rationalization experienced outside the bureaucracies of agriculture. "The concentration of the farmland into larger and larger holdings and fewer hands—with the consequent increase of overhead, debt, and dependence on machines--is a matter of complex significance . . . . It forces a profound revolution in the farmer's mind: once his investment in land and machines is large enough, he must forsake the values of husbandry and assume those of finance and technology. Thenceforth his thinking is not determined by agricultural responsibility, but by financial accountability and the capacities of machines. . . . He is caught up in the drift of energy and interest away from the land. Production begins to override maintenance. The economy of money has infiltrated and subverted the economies of nature, energy, and the human spirit" (Berry 1977, 45-46).

A society that defines immediate productivity, efficiency and profit as ultimate value—that judges all by these standards—cannot afford concern for tradition, environment, or wider social concern. The removal of human values from production, an activity that defines our very humanity, affects all areas of our lives. It leaves us cut off from our past, cut off from wider moral and social values, cut off from our humanity itself. "It is impossible to mechanize production without mechanizing consumption, impossible to make machines of soil, plants, and animals without making machines also of people" (Berry 1977, 75). And again: "If human values are removed from production, how can they be preserved in consumption? How can we value our lives if we devalue them in making a living?" (Berry 1977, 79). Modern bureaucracies, modern thought (zweckrational), promote continued intensification, implying infinite industrial growth and consumption. But considering wider cultural and ecological values, Berry argues, leads one to restraint. These wider concerns, however, are not given voice in our bureaucracies, are not given value in our culture.

Chapter 3: Oligarchy

If voting changed anything, they'd make it illegal.

--Emma Goldman

In 1915, Robert Michels, a sociologist and friend of Max Weber, formulated the "iron law of oligarchy." According to this iron law "It is organization which gives birth to the dominion of the elected over the electors,...of the delegates over the delegators. Who says organization, says oligarchy" (365). The reason for this association is that any large scale organization is faced with problems that can only be solved by creating a bureaucracy. A bureaucracy, in turn, must be hierarchically organized; the effective functioning of an organization requires the concentration of power in the hands of a few people at the top of the organization. In effect, this separates individuals from control over the decisions that affect their lives. All societies with any degree of large scale organization are therefore elitist. Elitism is not the result of conspiracies, or general voter apathy, it is endemic to social organization. While all societies are elitist, the power of elites varies across societies and through time. The fact that those on top of modern bureaucratic hierarchies can command vast resources in pursuit of their interests gives them great social, economic, and political power. To discuss the future without reference to the power and interests of these elites is to engage in empty academic exercise.

By its very nature, bureaucracy generates an enormous degree of social power. Great power in America is concentrated in a tiny handful of people. A few thousand individuals out of 220 million Americans decide about war and peace, wages and prices, consumption and investment, employment and production, law and justice, taxes and benefits, education and learning, health and welfare, advertising and communication, life and leisure (Dye 1983, 3). While democratic theory has it that government is ultimately responsible to the people, government bureaucracies have grown so large, so numerous, and so complex that this accountability is largely illusionary. The problem is further compounded in West by huge corporations, economic bureaucracies that have tremendous impact on our lives, an impact over which we have little control.

Centralization and Enlargement

The centralization of power has been accelerating in the twentieth century. At the turn of the century, two-thirds of all government expenditures were accounted for by state and local governments; today, they account for only one-third. Today's economy is about 20 times larger than it was in 1900, but total government expenditures are 65 times larger. The federal government alone spends approximately 23 percent of the nation's Gross National Product. Corporate concentration has also been intensifying. "The long-established norm of market structure and behavior is that of oligopoly, that is, the constrained rivalry of a few interdependent sellers who compete mainly by means of product differentiation" (Dye 1983, 29).

While the trend toward oligopoly was well advanced in the earlier part of this century, after World War II, the pace of centralization quickened. With most of the other industrial powers crippled by the war, American manufacturing companies grew to phenomenal size. As a result, by 1975, the 200 largest manufacturing companies had a greater share of all manufacturing, sales, employment, and assets than the largest 500 had in 1955 (Harris 1979). "Economic power in America is highly concentrated. ...America's 500 largest corporations—"the Fortune 500"—collectively take in about $7.2 trillion in revenues each year, and these corporations collectively control about $18 trillion in total assets. These 500 corporations account for roughly 60 percent of all corporate revenues and all corporate assets in the nation" (Dye 1999, 13-14).

Coincidental with the centralization of economic power is its enlargement in the modern world. The key decision makers have instruments to influence the masses, such as television, advertising and public relations firms, and techniques of propaganda that are unsurpassed in the history of mankind. In addition, the means of power and violence are now infinitely greater. Finally, the tremendous advances in transportation and communication have made it much more likely that the elite can coordinate this power. Not only do these developments place more power in the hands of the elites, it makes the decisions of the elite more consequential. Elites exercise considerable influence on public opinion through foundations, associations such as the Council on Foreign Relations and the Business Advisory Council, and elite universities. "In short, the institutional structure of our society (and the people at the top of that structure) encourages the development of some kinds of public issues, but prevents other kinds of issues from ever being considered by the American public" (Dye 1983, 8). Through the domination of key institutions, the elite are able to shape the framework within which American opinion is formed.

The Power Elite

C. Wright Mills published *The Power Elite* in 1956. According to Mills, the power elite consist of key persons in the three major institutions of modern society: the corporations, the federal government, and the military. Together these people form a unified elite that, while not omnipotent, is formidable. "They occupy the strategic command posts of the social structure, in which are now centered the effective means of power and wealth and the celebrity which they enjoy" (Mills 1956, 4). The elite are those few who have formal authority over these large institutions which shape our lives. Through their institutional positions, the power elite control the key bureaucracies in American social life. Power is thus an attribute of social organization, not of individuals.

By asserting that there is a Power Elite in American society, Mills is not asserting that there is a self-conscious ruling class that is cynically manipulating the masses. It is not a conspiracy of "evil men," but rather a social structure that has first enlarged and centralized the means of decision and power and, second, placed this power in the hands of men of similar social background and outlook. Dye (2002) divides American society into ten dominant sectors: (1) industrial corporations, (2) banking, (3) insurance, (4) investments, (5) mass media, (6) law, (7) education, (8) foundations, (9) civic and cultural organizations, (10) government (10-11). Dye defined elite individuals who held formal positions of authority over the largest corporate institutions, as well as those officers of elite law firms, well-endowed private universities, major philanthropic foundations, and civic and cultural organizations. Finally, in the government sector he identified 284 individuals who occupy formal positions of authority in the federal government (cabinet officers, party leaders, Supreme Court Justices) (9-10). In all, Dye identifies about 7,300 positions at the top of his twelve sectors. The reason there are so few is that economic power in America is highly concentrated.

"Indeed, only about 4,500 individuals—two one-thousands of 1 percent of the population—exercise formal authority over half of the nation's industrial assets, over half of all banking assets, over half of all assets in communications, transportation, and utilities, and over two thirds of all insurance assets. These individuals are the presidents, officer-directors, and directors of the largest corporations in these fields. The reason for this concentration of economic power in the hands of so few people is found in the concentration of industrial and financial assets in a small number of giant corporations. . . . There are about 200,000 industrial corporations in the United States with total assets in 1980 of about 1.2 trillion. The largest 100 corporations control 55.0 percent ($683 billion) of all industrial assets. . . . Concentration in transportation, communication, and utilities is even greater than in industry. Fifty corporations out of 67,000 in these fields control over two-thirds of the nation's assets in airlines, railroads, communications, and electricity and gas. . . . The financial world is equally concentrated. The 50 largest banks out of 17,700 serving the nation control 61.3 percent of all banking assets. . . . In the insurance field, 50 companies out of 1,890 control over 75 percent of all insurance assets" (Dye 1983, 20).

Even the estimate of 4,500 individuals at the top of these hierarchies is inflated. Dye includes the board of directors as being at the top of these hierarchies. While the average number of board members in the largest 100 industrial corporations is fourteen, their control is largely illusionary. With the "managerial revolution," in which professional managers displace owners as corporate decision makers, the number of men controlling corporate bureaucracies is actually much smaller.

In Mills's view, major national power now resides almost exclusively in the economic, the political, and the military domains. "All other institutions have been diminished in scope and power and made subordinate to the 'big three.' Families and churches and schools adapt to modern life; governments and armies and corporations shape it; and, as they do so, they turn these lesser institutions into means for their ends. . . . And the symbols of these lesser institutions are used to legitimate the power and the decisions of the big three" (Mills 1956, 6).

Schools have become appendages of corporations and government, sorting and training the young for their corporate careers, inculcating patriotism, respect for authority, and the glories of capitalism along the way. Families have lost their political and productive functions;

they now serve largely as consumption units as well as suppliers of workers and soldiers to the bureaucratic-industrial state. While families are still major socialization agents of the young, they now share this function with schools and the mass media. Through the socialization process each of us comes to accept the system as it is. There is a general consensus on what is right and "natural." The interests of the elites become legitimized. "The interests of an economically dominant class never stand naked. They are enshrouded in the flag, fortified by the law, protected by the police, nurtured by the media, taught by the schools, and blessed by the church" (Parenti 1978, 84). Mills points out that churches regularly supply chaplains to improve the morale and thus the fighting efficiency of our armed forces. More recent examples would include the rise of the religious right in America, with its heavy emphasis on political patriotism, military power, and hostility toward programs of public welfare. All of these trends serve to legitimate and strengthen the power and authority of the big three.

It is their similar social background that provides one of the major sources of unity among the elite. The bulk of the elite, Mills asserts, come from the upper third of the income and occupational pyramids. They are closely knit through intermarriages, private preparatory schools, Ivy League colleges, and very exclusive gentlemen's clubs. Non-upper class members of the elite consist of hired corporate managers, experts, and corporate lawyers--men who are competent technocrats.

In his book *Who Rules America?*, G. William Domhoff (1967) demonstrates that the majority of leaders of the executive branch are either members of the upper class or former employees of institutions controlled by members of the upper class. He traces the occupants of various government positions and finds that members of the elite dominate the President's Cabinet, especially in the Departments of State, Treasury, Defense, Commerce, and even Labor. For example, "of the 13 men who have been Secretary of Defense or Secretary of War since 1932, eight have been listed in the Social Register. The others are bankers and corporation executives, and clearly members of the power elite" (99). Domhoff also documents the upper class/power elite credentials of the Diplomatic Corps, the inner circles of presidential advisors and emissaries, and the Regulatory Agencies. Where Domhoff cannot document upper class domination, such as in the federal judiciary, he does find evidence of considerable influence by the upper class. Dye (2002) also reports on the elite credentials of the executive branch: "What is even more impressive is the fact that 54 percent of the corporate leaders and 42 percent of the governmental leaders are graduates of twelve heavily endowed, prestigious 'name' private universities—Harvard, Yale, Chicago, Stanford, Columbia, M.I.T., Cornell, Northwestern, Princeton, Johns Hopkins, Pennsylvania, and Dartmouth. Elites in America are notably Ivy League" (148). Top federal bureaucrats, corporation executives and directors, and the leaders of all sectors of society are drawn from the upper-middle-class sectors of the population. The recruitment of elites from the same social strata assures their unified world view.

Of the three sectors of institutional power, Mills implies that the corporate elite are perhaps the most powerful. But he asserts that the power elite cannot be understood as a mere reflection of economic elites; rather it is the (sometimes uneasy) alliance of economic, political, and military power. Most contemporary elite theorists tend to remove military personnel from full participation within the power elite. They point out that high-ranking military officers often have different class and regional backgrounds than members of government and business elites. Further, while some military leaders do manage to gain important corporate and governmental posts, it is not common. Most now see the military as being dominated by the executive branch of government. Even Mills focus changed from a military elite to militarism among America's elite in his later writings.

A second source of the unity of the power elite is the increasingly explicit coordination within and between corporate and governmental institutions. Since World War II, business and government have become increasingly intertwined. The executive branch of government has grown with regulatory agencies, commissions, and advisory councils that patrol, protect, and coordinate the complex national economy—agencies and commissions that are usually staffed by corporate men. Corporate and government planning have replaced the marketplace in many sectors of the American economy. Elite organizations such as the Council on Foreign Relations, the Business Roundtable, the Committee for Economic Development also provide coordination to national policy. "They bring together people in top positions from the corporate world, the universities, the law firms, and the government, to develop explicit policies and programs for submission to Congress, the President, and the nation" (Dye 1983, 150). While Mills does not claim that the coordination between elites is total, he does view it as an important source of the unity of the elite. "Just how close the resemblance between governmental and business officials may be is shown by the ease and frequency with which men pass form one hierarchy to another. While such changes may seem mere incidents in an individual career, the meaning of such interpenetration of managerial elite goes beyond this, modifying the meaning of the upper brackets and the objective functions of the several big organizations" (Mills 1951, 83).

Evidence of explicit coordination within the corporate sector is widespread. While Dye (2002, 139-142) has identified 7,314 top institutional positions in the 10 different sectors of society, these positions were occupied by only 5,778 individuals. In other words, 15 percent of Dye's identified elite held more than one elite position (many of the others also hold other corporate, government, and civic posts, but not top positions as defined by Dye). Because some individuals hold three or more top positions, approximately 32 percent of all elite positions identified by Dye are interlocked with other elite positions. He labels these interlockers as an "inner group" who hold multiple directorships of large corporate and financial institutions, as well as foundations, universities, and civic associations. Dye believes that their multiple positions encourage them to take a broad view of corporate problems. The inner group is in a position to coordinate the activities of a variety of bureaucratic organizations. "They move from the industrial point of interest and outlook to the interest and outlook of all big corporate property as a whole" (Mills 1956, 121).

Dye (2002) found little evidence of interlocking between corporate and government sectors of society. To the extent that high government officials are interlocked at all, it is with civic and cultural and educational institutions. It is within the corporate sector that interlocking is most prevalent. If there is a "coming together" of corporate, governmental, and military elites as C. Wright Mills contends, it does not appear to be by means of interlocking directorates" (Dye 1983, 189-190). This finding is not too surprising in that Dye identifies only 284 elite government positions, all top executive, military, judicial, and legislative officials of the federal government. Most are forbidden by law to serve on corporate boards. However, when Dye examines the leadership experience of the elite over a lifetime, the picture changes dramatically. There is a revolving door between government and the private sector. Nearly 40 percent of Dye's corporate elite held at least one government post at some time during their career. While Dye finds that only 10 percent of his identified government elites were recruited from the corporate world (61.5 percent were recruited from the legal profession), he does report that eleven of Reagan's cabinet officers (58 percent) have served as officers or directors of corporations, and eight officers (42 percent) are members of the Council on Foreign Relations. The power elite maintains its unity through the revolving door exchange of personnel between the corporate and government sectors of society, as well as the recruitment of all institutional elites from the same social strata.

Below the power elite, Mills saw two other levels of power in American society. At the bottom are the great masses of people—largely unorganized, ill informed, and virtually powerless. Controlled and manipulated from above, they are exploited economically and politically. Between the masses and the elite are the "middle levels" of power. Comprised of local opinion leaders and special interest groups, they neither represent the mass nor have any real effect on the elite. Mills saw the U.S. Congress as a reflection of this middle level of power. Although Congress decides some minor issues, the power elite ensure that no serious challenge to its control is tolerated in the political arena. More recent writings in the elitist tradition tend to credit Congress with more power than Mills' view. The power of Congress to block legislation, to force compromise, and to investigate the decisions of the executive branch are still considerable. "But Congress does not initiate policy; instead, it responds to the policy initiatives of others. Congress accepts, modifies, or rejects the policies and programs developed by the President and White House staff, executive departments, influential interest groups, and the mass media" (Dye 1983, 105). Political Action Committees (PACs) distribute money to legislators who support their interests. People of wealth often back a promising politician early in his career, sponsoring those who are sympathetic to their views. The parties, then, are constrained to choose candidates with views congruent with the economic elites. While most assert that corporations are among the most active and successful of all the lobbyists, few claim that Congress is completely dominated by corporate elites. Given recent trends in the amount of corporate money in lobbying and campaign finance, as well as government's inability to reign in corporate excess, this view is beginning to change.

The Corporate State

According to Michael Harrington (1976), the focus on the power elite may serve to understate the degree to which the very institutions of government, even when not under the direct influence of elites representing their class interests, will follow corporate priorities. Again and again, Harrington emphasizes that the modern state is not a mere tool of corporations, is not a conscious, conspiratorial phenomenon. The elites do not have an omniscient and objective sense of their interests; nor are they all powerful in achieving their goals. Rather, since the dominant economic institutions in modern society are private corporations, the government must follow corporate priorities. "The welfare-state government is not itself the initiator of most production within the economy. The corporations do that. However, that same government is increasingly charged with arranging the preconditions for profitable production. Its funds, its power, its political survival, depend on private sector performance. So do the jobs of most workers. The state's interest in perpetuating its own rule is thus, in economic fact, identified with the health of the capitalist economy" (Harrington 1976, 307).

Harrington gives numerous examples of how the modern state formulates social policies that benefit corporate America, often worsening (or creating) problems that the government then deplores. Agriculture, Harrington points out, is a sector dominated by gigantic agribusiness. In 1971, for example, nearly 80 percent of all agricultural income was received by only about 20 percent of the largest farms. By 2009 farms were even further concentrated with 10 percent of the farms controlling 80 percent of all farm production. These farms continue to receive tens of billions of dollars in federal subsidies, allowing large corporate agriculture to replace the independent farmer at enormous federal expense. It makes good political sense to fashion agricultural policy so as to benefit organizations with economic and political power.

A second example of the corporate priorities of the U.S. federal government reported by Harrington is centered on the federal highway system. "In an urbanized, interdependent society, the federally funded highways made great sense from the point of view of middle- and upper-class suburbia and the new plants and laboratories located on its fringes. Yet they were disastrous for the cities, the minorities, the poor, the mass transit system and the environment" (Harrington 1976, 324). Harrington also documents corporate bias in government policies concerning urban affairs, housing, and energy.

According to Harrington, the state promotes the economy through four actions. First, the state allows the formation of oligopolies, cartels, and multinationals to promote managerial planning and eliminate the vagaries of the market. Second, the government subsidizes technological innovation to create new needs and markets. Third, government subsidizes many private industries through massive defense spending. Finally, the state engages in direct intervention in the economy to offset inflation and recession/depression.

Dye inadvertently makes similar points when examining the structural interests of corporate and governmental elites. While admitting that his analysis provides strong evidence for the existence of a power elite, he attempts to make the elite appear non-threatening by claiming that elite goals are really America's goals (a perspective similar to the popularized "What's good for General Motors is good for the country"). He quotes John Kenneth Galbraith on the how non-threatening elite interests really are: "All have interests in a strong and growing economy, domestic tranquility, and constantly expanding military power. The state is strongly concerned with the stability of the economy. And with its expansion or growth. And with education. And with technical and scientific advance. And, most notably, with the national defense. These are the national goals; they are sufficiently trite so that one has a reassuring sense of the obvious in articulating them. All have their counterpart in the needs and goals of the techno-structure. It requires stability in demand for its planning. Growth brings promotion and prestige. It requires trained manpower. It needs government underwriting of research and development. Military and other technical procurement support its most developed form of planning. At each point the government has goals with which the techno-structure can identify itself" (Dye 1983, 58-59). But are goals centered on economic growth and militarism actually in the interests of the entire nation?

The structural interests of governmental and corporate elites lie in economic growth. It should be noted here that growth is not an inherent part of the industrial mode of production. The industrial mode of production consists of rational technologies and social practices for regulating the flow of energy from the environment. These rational principles are derived from science and observation and human reason. There is no inherent reason within the industrial mode of production to exclude the principles of ecology when fashioning our technologies and practices. Resistance to such innovations does not lie within the infrastructure of industrial society, but within structures and superstructures.

Part of the commitment to growth is inherent in the nature of capitalism itself. The development of capitalism predates the industrial revolution by some 100 years (Harrington 1976; Harris 1977). Under capitalism the distribution of most goods and services is carried out by 'companies' which control or have access to accumulated supplies of money or 'capital'. The object of such companies is to accumulate more capital and to do it as quickly and efficiently as possible by maximizing the rate of making profits. A company can increase its rate of profit if it gains a technological advantage over its competitors and lowers its unit cost. Technological innovation, therefore, soon becomes the key to the accumulation of capital and business success. Science, in turn, provides the key to technological innovation (Harris 1977, 262). The goals and drives of the capitalist class and their managers are therefore achieved through a growing economy. We measure the health of our economy (as well as the health of individual corporations that make up the national economy) by measures of growth. Increases in Gross National Product, productivity, and profitability are almost universally considered the national priority. Not only does this economic growth serve to further enrich the elite, it also serves to protect acquired wealth from the threat of redistribution.

The demands of the lower classes for increases in income have traditionally been met by increasing economic output. Even before Reagan, economic growth was seen as a way of "painlessly" addressing the needs of the under- and working-classes. Without economic growth these demands could not be addressed without open class warfare. "For under a stationary (or even slow-growing capitalism), continued efforts of the lower and middle classes to improve their positions can be met only by diminishing the absolute incomes of the upper echelons of society" (Heilbroner 1980, 102). Harrington makes a similar point: "It (the state) can, as long as production is expanding increase the absolute living standards of the masses; it cannot change the basic structure of inequality, for that is essential to the accumulation of capital—that is, to the survival and perpetuation of the system itself" (Harrington 1976, 318). Fundamental reform that challenges the existence of the elite simply cannot be granted. It is only by continuing economic expansion that the elite can "painlessly" maintain their positions.

In a society dominated by large corporations, policies of the federal government cannot run counter to the interests of the corporate sector "unless they have the support of a determined mass movement willing to fight for structural change" (Harrington 1976, 223). In the last fifty years we have seen the growth in the size and power of many interest groups aside from big business. Civil rights organizations, environmental groups, feminists, the Moral Majority, anti-nuclear movements, and more recently the Tea Party and the Occupy Wall Street movement (or the "99 Percent") have all arisen with their specific agendas. The modern state can be seen as the result of some compromise between these interest groups and the elite. Sometimes the goals of these interest groups are achieved because they do not directly conflict with the interests and goals of the elite. Other goals are attained because they ameliorate some of the worst abuses of corporate capitalism, reluctantly conceded by elites to head off revolutionary discontent. Finally, some of the goals of these interest groups directly conflict. Issues such as environmental protection, consumer and worker safety, and a return to a progressive tax structure will cost corporate America dearly. The elite resist these types of structural reforms using all available resources. The conflict over these issues is often intense and bitter. Both sides use science and propaganda to try to further their position. More often than not, because the state is systematically biased in favor of the elites, as well as the flood of money into the political system, the elites prevail. But at times, when the opposition is tightly organized, when the masses are sufficiently aroused, corporate elites must grant some reform. But even this is fleeting. For public attention and outrage is ephemeral; corporate interest is permanent. Matt Taibbi (2012) reports on the tactics that were used to stop financial reform after the 2008 economic collapse:

"The fate of Dodd-Frank over the past two years is an object lesson in the government's inability to institute even the simplest and most obvious reforms, especially if those reforms happen to clash with powerful financial interests. From the moment it was signed into law, lobbyists and lawyers have fought regulators over every line in the rulemaking process. Congressmen and presidents may be able to get a law passed once in a while—but they can no longer make sure it *stays* passed. You win the modern financial-regulation game by filing the most motions, attending the most hearings, giving the most money to the most politicians, and, above all, by keeping at it, day after day, year after fiscal year, until stealing is legal again. 'It's a scorched-earth policy,' says Michael Greenberger, a former regulator who was heavily involved with the drafting of Dodd-Frank. 'It requires constant combat. And it never, ever ends'" (para 4).

In a corporate dominated society there is a necessity to view environmental problems of depletion/pollution as manageable. Contrary evidence is denigrated and/or denied. Economic growth is presented as the solution to our environmental problems, not as one of the primary causes. Grudging reform of the worst environmental abuses are granted, but in the main, problems of environment are dealt with by appeals to further science and technology rather than fundamental structural and infrastructural change. This is not to say there is no alternative to the dominant view. As we will see in the following chapter, there is an alternative world view—but it is a world view in direct opposition to the structural interests of elites and, as such, is not likely to become dominant without true revolutionary change.

Chapter 4: The Politics of the Future

The important fact of the present time is not the struggle between capitalism and socialism but the struggle between industrial civilization and humanity.

--Bertrand Russell, (1872-1970)

This chapter examines the two diametrically opposed political positions regarding the future of industrial society by focusing on the exchange between the MIT *Limits to Growth* group, and the Sussex response to that work, *Models of Doom*. It is my contention that these two groups represent two opposing value orientations mirroring Weber's action typology: rational action in relation to a goal, and rational action in relation to broader human values. One of the most heated debates in futurist literature is over the ability of the natural environment to sustain continued population and industrial growth. According to the *Ecological Worldview*, continued population and industrial growth will inevitably reach the depletion/pollution limits of the natural environment, leading to the possible collapse of industrial society. Opposed to this is the *Technological Worldview* which holds that natural limits to growth are much less restrictive than the ecologists claim, and that the further development of technology can be expected to continue to overcome any existing depletion/pollution limits well into the foreseeable future. It is found that the value orientation of the researchers play a central role in their arguments and findings.

The ecological orientation expresses extreme dissatisfaction with modern political, economic, and social institutions—a dissatisfaction that goes well beyond environmentalism. The technological orientation is the worldview of the elites of industrial-bureaucratic societies thus it is the dominant world view of our age. The ecological orientation is attacked from both left and right because the argument that industrial growth is not sustainable challenges the very foundation of capitalist as well as socialist societies. The environmental debate can only be fully understood as a political debate over the control of the future.

There is a long-ranging debate among physical and social scientists over the ability of the planet to sustain industrial and population growth. The purpose of this chapter is to examine critically the social and political values underlying both sides of the debate, for the debate over environmental limits is not limited to the realm of objective science. Rather, the debate is part of a larger conflict of structural interests and superstructural values, a conflict that is complicated by the fact that it cuts across traditional ideological lines. The debate is over the future, and the two sides of the debate have very different conceptions of what is both attainable and desirable.

Perhaps the most exhaustive series of studies of environmental constraints to infrastructural growth were conducted by the MIT System Dynamics Group under the auspices of the Club of Rome. In the late 1960s, the Club of Rome, an informal organization of scientists, educators, economists, industrialists, and non-elected government officials from many countries, initiated a project on "The

Predicament of Mankind." The purpose of this project was to examine the complex social problems of all nations. These problems included the infrastructural problems of depletion and pollution; the structural problems of poverty, urbanization, unemployment, inflation and other economic disruptions; and superstructural problems such as alienation and the rejection of traditional values. The predicament of mankind, according to the Club of Rome, is not the simple summation of these problems, but rather our failure to grasp their interrelationships and significance.

It is the failure to analyze these problems in terms of the entire world system that leads to our inability to devise effective responses to our current crises. The first phase of the project focused on the intensification of the infrastructure and its impact on the global environment. Under the direction of Professor Dennis Meadows, a research team constructed a global model (World 3) that attempts to simulate the interaction of five processes: (1) growing population, (2) industrial production, (3) agricultural production, (4) depletion of natural resources, and (5) pollution of the environment. A computer simulation model built along the system dynamics methodology pioneered by Jay Forrester (the creator of World 1 and 2), the World 3 model is fundamentally a theory of how change occurs in social systems. The underlying theory of the model is that infrastructural intensification has impact on the environment (in the form of depletion and pollution) which, in turn, has reciprocal impact on further infrastructural intensification. The value of the model does not lie in precise prediction but in its ability to simulate the interactions of growing population, production, and the environment under a variety of assumptions. Thus the model is designed to project present trends into the future as well as to evaluate the potential impact of change in the social system. The results of their studies have been published in the popular press (*The Limits to Growth*, 1972), as well as technical reports written for a professional audience (*Toward Global Equilibrium: Collected Papers*, 1973; and *Dynamics of Growth in a Finite World*, 1974). There was also a follow-up, The Limits to Growth: The 30 Year Update (2004) which I will be referring to as well.

In 1972, the MIT System Dynamics Group (hereafter identified as the MIT group or simply MIT) presented their preliminary work to several research groups around the world. Their stated purpose was to encourage critical analysis of the World 3 model and its underlying assumptions. One group that responded with vigor was the Sussex Policy Research Unit at Sussex University (hereafter the Sussex group or Sussex). Their comments on the World 3 model, as well as a response by the MIT group were subsequently published in *Models of Doom: A Critique of the Limits of Growth* in 1973. The Sussex critique focused on four broad areas of the MIT studies: (1) the estimates of physical limits, (2) the failure of MIT to incorporate social values in the World 3 model, (3) the failure to incorporate technological advance into World 3, and (4) the values of the MIT group and their influence on the analysis. The first three issues raised by Sussex will be incorporated in the detailed description of the structure and simulations of the World 3 model in subsequent chapters.

The discussion of values, of both MIT and Sussex, will be discussed in this chapter.

There is substantial accord between the underlying theory of the World 3 model and the infrastructural-environmental relationships posited by materialists. Most importantly, the MIT group and sociocultural materialism share a pronounced systems view. "But the most important part of our worldview, the part that is least commonly shared, is our systems perspective. ...We see the many elements of demography, economy, and the environment as one planetary system, with innumerable interactions. We see stocks and flows and feedbacks and thresholds in the interconnections, all of which influence the way the system will behave in the future and influence the actions we might take to change its behavior" Meadows, Randers, and Meadows 2004, Kindle Locations 422-429).

Both sociocultural materialism and the World 3 model explicitly recognize the environment as the foundation of sociocultural systems. Society must ultimately exist within the constraints imposed by its environment. Both consider the mode of production and reproduction the means by which society adapts to these physical limits. Both recognize that infrastructural growth can affect environmental limits through depletion and pollution. Materialists specifically point to the intensification-depletion/pollution process as the engine of sociocultural evolution. The World 3 model maintains that both depletion and pollution are limiting factors that will necessitate large scale sociocultural change, again this is consistent with the materialist position which claims that all major structural and superstructural change is rooted in the relationships between the infrastructure and the environment. While the World 3 model itself is limited to infrastructural processes, the research team assumes structural and superstructural changes when evaluating technological and social policies designed to bring infrastructural growth under social control. Finally, both the empirical model and the theory are nondeterministic. While the limitations imposed by the environment are the parameters around which the entire sociocultural system must adapt, there are a range of possible adaptations.

The Sussex group quite rightly maintains that any model of a social system involves assumptions about the workings of that system, assumptions that are necessarily biased by the values of the modelers. This is especially true when considering areas where information is scarce or when attempting to extrapolate trends into the future. "The mental model one chooses to describe the real world (especially the human world) is an inextricable part of one's values, interests, hopes and fears. This still applies even when the mental model is translated into a computer program" (Cole 1973, 133). The Sussex group characterizes the values of the MIT group as "neo-Malthusian" combined with a "strong preoccupation with environmental issues characteristic of contemporary American thought" (Cole 1973, 9). In tracing the roots of this preoccupation with environmental issues, the Sussex group draws a sharp contrast between two world views-one based on environmentalism and one based on technological progress. Both world views are based on different images of man and society; both have unique visions of a desirable future.

This rather neat dichotomy of a technological and ecological world view is complicated by ideological considerations—both world views cut across traditional ideological lines. Both have their proponents and critics on the right and the left of the political spectrum, though in recent years this has changed. While the MIT group is clearly on the left (favoring a redistribution of wealth, social control of the means of production, long range government planning, etc.), other advocates of an ecological world view exhibit marked conservative tendencies (Malthus himself could be classified as a political reactionary). The Sussex group, advocates of the technological world view, "included people of very diverse political views, ranging across the whole spectrum from Conservative to Marxist, and some of no identifiable political complexion" (Cole 1973, 9-10). Since the Sussex critique is divided into chapters that are written by individuals with little coordination between them, the critique tends to attack the environmental movement in general and the MIT group in particular on all fronts. Consequently, there are numerous contradictions. The environmental movement is portrayed as a tool of the wealthy in one chapter and an ally of the radical left in others. Despite these contradictions, what emerges is a description of an ecological movement that is sympathetic to many leftist and rightest critiques of industrial society, but suspicious of simple structural solutions.

The Radical Critique

The attack from the left castigates the ecological world view as an elitist position that is concerned with preservation of amenities and problems of leisure. It is faulted for ignoring "the economic, political and moral problems of using the world's resources in a more equitable and effective manner. . ."(Cole 1973, 157). Because it is hostile to economic growth, the environmental movement can be seen as supporting the status quo and thus the materially well off. Their hostility to economic growth, Sussex maintains, can be used to put restrictions of the kinds of technology supplied to third world countries through economic aid. "By reducing the consumption of raw materials in the industrial countries, the third world countries would suffer. This is not to argue that there is no ground for concern about the environment, nor that present patterns of economic growth are the right ones. Nor is it to suggest that all parts of the environment movement are the natural allies of the well-off; radical political movements have clearly played an important role. Nor again is it to suggest that all materially well-off environmentalists are concerned with their personal interests. It is simply to say that, in the movement to improve the environment and to stop economic growth, there may often be some confusion between the general interest and the interests of a specific, materially well-off group, and that Forrester and Meadows make some appeal to this group" (Cole 1973, 155). Sussex maintains that the idealism that was once focused on problems of mal-distribution is being shifted to environmental concerns, making it more likely that the poor will continue to be ignored.

The second part of the radical critique of the American ecology movement is that it has mistakenly attributed many of the excesses of capitalism to industry and technology in general. The leftist members of the Sussex group assert that the ecology movement began in the U.S. because the American government, unlike the governments of Europe, has identified itself too closely with capitalism. European governments view capitalism as an asset to be managed in the interests of the nation. American government, on the other hand, has been slow to regulate the "harmful side-effects" of economic growth, or to establish either long-range government planning or many of the basic social services long familiar in Europe. The ecology movement blames industrialism and technology for much of the pollution and degradation of the environment. "Another possible interpretation is that the unbridled pursuit of private gain rather than industry and technology per se has been the main problem. In this case alternative institutional arrangements might be expected to resolve some of the problems" (Cole 1973, 182).

There is some truth and much hyperbole in the leftist critique of the ecology movement. The truth lies in the assertion that one wing of the ecology movement is concerned with the preservation of the status quo. The hyperbole lies in extending the goals and values of this wing to the ecology movement as a whole. The MIT group points out that far from shifting the focus of man away from problems of structure, a fully developed ecological world view draws attention to the interdependence of all components of the social system: "Human societies will not achieve a more equitable distribution of wealth until they better understand the processes of growth. Historically at least, growth of population and capital has been correlated with the concentration of wealth and with rising gaps in the absolute income of the rich and poor . . . (B)y relying on the false promises of growth, social institutions are able to delay facing the very important and difficult task of making social trade-offs and defining social goals. Until these tasks are squarely faced there will be no redistribution of income" (cited in Cole 1973, 236-237).

Many traditional leftists are hostile to the ecology movement not because they fear it will siphon off popular concern for many structural problems, but because it labels purely structural solutions to these problems as wholly inadequate. There is also some truth to the assertion that the ecology movement has inadvertently attributed many problems of capitalism to industrialism (the reverse criticism could easily be made of many traditional Marxists). The MIT group never directly addresses the relative weight it gives to problems of capitalism and problems of industrialism. The MIT critique of capitalism is rarely overt, veiled in the language of ecology rather than politics. Part of the problem lies in the pragmatic bent of American ideology; part of it is rooted in the nation's hostility toward the left. But the absence of leftist rhetoric does not mean that MIT has not been influenced by radical analysis. That the MIT group views the "unbridled pursuit of private gain" as a major problem is readily apparent in their description of the "equilibrium state" designed to bring physical growth under social control. Their "solution" combines many principles of ecology with many structural reforms long advocated by the left. However, unlike the traditional left, they view industrialism and the material value system that it promotes as an intricate part of the current crisis.

The radical critique of the ecology movement would have more validity if it could be demonstrated that: (1) the ecology movement is dominated by right-wing forces, (2) man can only be concerned with only one burning social issue at a time, or (3) an ecological world view is incompatible with the left. Other members of the Sussex group make it clear that none of these assertions are tenable. In fact, they claim that it is the leftist values of the ecology movement that have unduly influenced MIT's conclusions.

The Conservative Critique

The conservative analysis of the ecological world view offered by Sussex maintains that the socialist component of the environmental movement is much more pronounced than traditional radicals or environmentalists are willing to admit. "Much of the moral idealism which in earlier times found expression in various movements of social reform appears now, particularly in the USA, to seek an outlet in the environmentalist movement" (Cole 1973, 175). While it is the environmentalist critique of industrialism that is explicitly expressed by the ecology movement in general and the World 3 model in particular, the socialist critique of the cupidity of capitalism is also covertly expressed. "(T)he ideal of a more just and less selfish social arrangement is an important influence, particularly on Meadows, but this emerges as a bonus from the stable state, and not as its primary justification. The necessity for a stable state is overtly argued not on moral grounds but on the grounds of the physical impossibility of the continuation of economic growth. . . . The fact, however, that not only is pollution of the air by dust, chemicals noise, water and land resources listed, but also moral pollution, alienation and anomie, indicate that in many arguments environmental degradation is used as the basis for a questioning of economic and technical progress which derives from wider concerns and motives" (Cole 1973, 176-177).

"The ecology movement (and the MIT group) has combined the environmentalists' hostility to modern technology with the socialists' critique of the avarice and greed of capitalism to produce a broad attack on the values, structure, and infrastructure of modern industrial society. The appeal of the MIT report, as well as much of the appeal of the ecology movement in general, is based on a skepticism of both technology and the ability of present day institutions to control its use. It is connected with a general feeling of unease about the future of industrial society. This disillusion with the healing properties of capitalism has combined with a generalized and widespread feeling of despair at the apparent breakdown of certain societal values. Concern over rising crime rates, decline in the environment, changing family structure and relationships have all contributed to a general feeling of unease. It is as if society was on the verge, or perhaps even in the first phase of, some kind of vast social or cultural revolution whose exact nature has not yet been understood but of which people see premonitions all around them" (Cole 1973: 203).

Another member of the Sussex team characterized this general feeling of unease as "a widespread millennial mood, a sense that the advanced societies have over-reached themselves and unleashed forces which can no longer be controlled" (Cole 1973, 214). The ecological world view gives structure and voice to many of these concerns.

The leftist influence on the ecology movement is readily apparent in their description of possible futures. Environmental disasters and conflict is not their only warning. "The real thrust of their message is clear. Once the stable state has been achieved all the anxieties, frustrations and conflict engendered by the frantic endeavor to accumulate goods will have disappeared. Man will be able to realize the spiritual side of his nature. Rivers and lakes will be clean, population controlled, urban problems resolved. The golden age will begin. In common with other chiliasts, the new scientific chiliasts are utopians at heart. Like the great prophet of world salvation through world breakdown, Karl Marx, their apocalyptic visions of the immediate future are tempered by the glittering image of utopia barely discernible through the fire and brimstone that rages in the historical foreground. This is not to denigrate the beliefs of the Forrester/Meadows school in any sense; rather, it is to suggest that they too, despite the surface appearance of scientific neutrality and objectivity, bring us a message which can only be fully understood in the context of their own beliefs, values, assumptions and goals" (Cole 1973, 207).

The ecological left does share much with the traditional Marxist. But they differ from the Marxists in that they have abandoned the faith in technology (in varying degrees) as the means to a more just and equitable society. But there are other, more subtle differences between traditional Marxism and the ecological left. The ecological worldview leads many of its proponents to be somewhat more sympathetic to the conservative concern for the breakdown of traditional structures and values. There is also more suspicion toward both bureaucracy and centralization as viable institutional alternatives. Despite these differences, however, many of the values of the ecological left are leftist values.

While the conservative critique has focused on the leftist influence on the ecology movement, it has not adequately stressed their complementary relationship. In large part, the leftist critique of capitalism in the U.S. is consistent with ecological movement and its unique world view. The hostility toward the industrial system's exploitation and degradation of the earth is easily broadened toward capitalism and its exploitation and degradation of people. How could a movement hostile to the unrestrained use of technology fail to become concerned with the institutions that promote its abuse (unrestrained capitalism) and institutions that can possibly control it in the future (government)? How could such a movement fail to note the social disasters (as well as the physical) associated with industrial growth, particularly when that movement's world view is predicated on the interconnections between the environment and the various components of the social system? This is not to say that there are no conservative ecologists; to paraphrase Sussex, conservatives and reactionaries have clearly played a role in the environmental movement. What is being claimed, however, is that there is a natural affinity between an ecological world view and the radical critique of capitalism (an affinity that does not always operate in reverse).

The Sussex group is essentially correct in asserting that the ecological critique of industrial society cannot be fully understood without reference to the radical critique of social structure and values. The radical critique is an inextricable part of the MIT group's world view. Rather than exerting "undue influence," however, the two perspectives serve to reinforce one another. The validity of the charge that leftist values have unduly influenced the MIT analysis depends on our judgment of how adequately the assumptions of the World 3 model reflect physical reality. The World 3 model as presented in the Limits of Growth runs 10 different simulations of infrastructural – environmental relations using a variety of estimates of physical limits. The Sussex group considers all these posited limits to be unduly pessimistic. Yet, in no instance are these limits ever estimated to be the "worst possible case." For example, their 250 years' estimate for mineral reserves must assume a substantial degree of substitutability between minerals with lower identified reserves and those with higher indices. Because of the uncertain nature of these estimates, they use more optimistic estimates of reserves in subsequent simulations. They estimate that technology can improve land yields up to three times their present levels. The estimates of the harmful effects of persistent pollutants allows levels to rise up to 10 times their 1970 levels before the environment is seriously impaired. Further, they consistently estimate that technological improvement can extend all of these limits—in fact they maintain that this technological improvement is essential in order to achieve a stable society. However, they see economic and social costs in developing and deploying these technologies and they do not foresee technology as being able to overcome physical limits. This is not unduly pessimistic; this is in accordance with the laws of thermodynamics.

But it is on this basis that Sussex and others have labeled the MIT group as "pessimists." By calling their simulations "pessimistic" Sussex is implying that MIT's values have biased their research. But perspectives and values are not formed out of thin air. They are based on an individual's interpretation of the world around him. The MIT estimates and assumptions, while reflecting the worldview of the ecological left, are based on physical laws (particularly entropy) and observed relationships (the physical, economic, and social costs of technology, diminishing returns of technological improvement). The charge of *undue* influence can legitimately be made only when it can be demonstrated that the researcher's perspective and values have caused them to ignore inconvenient empirical facts or change these facts to suit their assumptions. Sussex has failed to make this case.

What Sussex has demonstrated, however, is that the debate over the environment is not conducted in the pure scientific realm of logic and reason. Sussex laid bare the value orientation of much of the environmental debate. The traditional left and right are both based on a technological world view—an intensifying mode of production, increasingly efficient technology, and greater material abundance. That technology can continue to offset depletion/pollution is a belief critical to capitalism and socialism alike. Both left and right, socialism and capitalism are essentially industrial economic theories that rely on the continued development of the mode of production. The ecological world view attacks the feasibility of continued intensification and is thus open to attack from both the traditional left and right. Even more important, by challenging the ideologies that support the industrial mode of production and its further intensification, the ecological worldview directly challenges the substantive interests of economic and government elites that benefit most from the status quo. Therefore, these elites and the institutions that they control view ecology as anathema.

In response to Sussex, the MIT group drew a contrast between the two competing world views: "The most important difference between the two groups is the underlying perception of man's place in the global system. Sussex believes that man can and should master nature for his own short-term needs. We suggest that man's tenure on earth will be longer if he can learn to formulate his goals and manage his affairs so that short- term solutions do not decrease long-term options" (Cole 1973, 218).

There is another difference between the two world views that plays a significant role in debates over the future. Clearly, MIT not only questions whether man *can* continue to exploit nature for profit, but also whether he *should* continue to do so. The ecological world-view fosters a deep distrust of technology. This distrust goes beyond assertions that technology alone cannot solve

97

environmental problems. Rooted in their systems view (you cannot do *one* thing), there is the belief that technology cannot be employed without creating further social inequalities. While technologists tend to rhapsodize over innovations, pointing out not only their efficiency but also their positive impact on human dignity (often defined as freedom from labor), popular power, and freedom, ecologists tend to view these same innovations as restricting human freedom, placing more power into the hands of the already powerful, and ultimately destroying human dignity. It is these differences in world views that underlie the contemporary debates over the future of industrial society. It is in the resolution of this struggle between two competing world views that the future of industrial society will be decided. The technological worldview, with its support of elites and the status-quo, currently dominates society. This worldview fosters continued infrastructural intensification in the belief that technology will find a way to tap into infinite resources for human consumption, that technology will find a way to clean up the mess. "Consequently, the modern person lives without constraint. He assumes, as he has clearly been taught to assume, that as a member of the human race he is sovereign in the universe. He assumes that there is nothing that he can do that he should not do, nothing that he can use that he should not use. His 'success'—which at present is indisputable—is that he has escaped any order that might imply restraints or impose limits" (Berry 1977, 53-54). But the escape from natural limits, Berry and other ecologists assert, can only be temporary. "Much as we long for infinities of power and duration, we have no

98

evidence that these lie within our reach. It is more likely that we will have either to live within our limits, within the human definition, or not live at all" (Berry 1977, 94).

Chapter 5: Environmental Limits

When one tugs at a single thing in nature, he finds it attached to the rest of the world.

--John Muir, (1838-1914)

The machine does not isolate man from the great problems of nature but plunges him more deeply into them.

--Antoine de Saint-Exupery

Any work addressing the future of industrial society must address the physical limits that constrain social systems, for any rapidly intensifying mode of production will face a common problem. "The increment in energy invested per unit time in production will inevitably overburden the self-renewing, self-cleansing capacity of the ecosystem. Regardless of which mode of production is involved, there is only one means of avoiding the catastrophic consequences of declining efficiencies: to shift to more efficient technologies. For the past 500 years western scientific technology has been competing against the most rapidly and relentlessly intensifying system of production in the history of our species" (Harris 1977, 271). Under such conditions, if a society is unable to develop and employ more efficient technologies or technologies that allow it to tap previously unused resources, it overshoots environmental carrying capacity and faces collapse. If new technology is successfully employed, it is only a matter of time until it too comes up against environmental limits of depletion and pollution. It is a continuous process; the race is never over; it can never be finally won.

Perhaps the most "popular" work predicting the inevitable collapse of industrial society is *Entropy: A New World View*, by Jeremy Rifkin (1980). Rifkin's views on the problems facing further infrastructural intensification are similar to the conclusions reached by the World 3 model. However, Rifkin has arrived at his conclusions from a very different route. Rather than relying on the simulations of a mathematical model of the interrelationships between population, production, and environment, Rifkin uses (some would say misuses) the concept of entropy to explain our present crisis and probable future.

The entropy law is the second law of thermodynamics and is considered by Rifkin to be the supreme law of the universe—a law that governs natural as well as social processes. The first law of thermodynamics states that all energy in the universe is constant; it cannot be created or destroyed. Only its form can change, never its essence. The second law, the entropy law, states that energy can only be changed in one direction, that is, from ordered to disordered, or from usable to unusable. Anytime we use energy on earth, a portion of that energy is lost forever. Entropy is a measure of the amount of energy no longer capable of conversion to human use. Another name for this dissipated energy and matter is pollution. Since energy and matter can neither be created nor destroyed but only transformed, and since it can only be transformed in one direction—toward an unusable state, depletion and pollution are an integral part of all life processes. The speed of the entropy process on earth, however, depends on the mode of production and reproduction of societies.

The further growth of the infrastructures of these societies will inevitably lead to the rapid depletion and pollution of our environment and the ultimate collapse of industrial societies.

Rifkin asserts that the entropy law destroys the notion that science and technology can create a more ordered world; in fact, he asserts the direct opposite. The application of technology to the production of food and goods is done at the expense of creating disorder in the environment. This is because technology can never create energy or matter; technology can only transform it from its naturally ordered state to pollution and waste. The larger and more complex the technology, the faster this transforming process occurs. Since each human being needs energy in order to survive, population growth also increases the speed of the entropy process.

Rifkin points out that it took millions of years (and probable climatic changes) for hunters and gatherers to deplete their environment. It took thousands of years for agricultural society to do the same. After only 100 years of intensive industrialism, however, the world is fast running out of many nonrenewable resources. Billions of years of stored solar energy in the form of oil and coal have been depleted. The ultimate depletion of other raw materials essential for industrial development is also in sight. And the resulting pollution of the planet is as deadly to life as it is appalling to our senses.

Throughout the book Rifkin denigrates technological solutions to the depletion and pollution process. Synfuels, nuclear fission and fusion are all portrayed as requiring immense capital inputs and serious technological difficulties in their development, and involving numerous safety and ecological problems in their use. Even if these problems could be solved, he maintains, the use of these alternatives would only speed up the entropy process. In Rifkin's view, technological fixes cannot work because technology must operate within the laws of thermodynamics. The ultimate collapse of industrial society is assured, however, by his view that the industrial infrastructure cannot be modified to fit environmental constraints.

Rifkin's assertion of the inability of industrial society to modify its social practices and technologies in order to fit into the environment permeates the book. The intensifying depletion and pollution of our planet will lead to the ultimate collapse of industrial society. In Rifkin's view, there simply is no choice, and several times he cautions of the futility of trying to change this future. "What the pragmatists cannot comprehend is that the Entropy Law is the ultimate scientific law governing the physical world, not a tool that can be used to patch up the old system . . . . (T)he pragmatist will turn his attention to defining the 'right' kind of growth, not realizing that the Entropy Law reveals to us that 'growth' is really a decrease in the world's wealth, nothing more than a process to take usable energy and transform it into an unusable state. Entropy shows us that the more an economy grows, the more it digs itself into a hole" (Rifkin 1980, 246).

This futility of change is a curious assertion, in many ways contradictory to the implicit structural model that Rifkin uses to analyze social change. His views on social structure and change are similar to the materialist paradigm. It is a view that stresses technological innovation and structural change out of environmental necessity. "(T)he great changes occurred (the agricultural and industrial revolutions) not as a result of the building up of abundance but as a result of the dissipation of resources" (Rifkin 1980, 65). His analysis of recent structural change stresses the growth of secondary organizations in order to coordinate and control recent infrastructural development. He asserts that the way man perceives his world is greatly influenced by the mode of production. The worldview dominant in the West since industrialization has become dominant has been one of progress and material abundance. But as the environmental crisis tightens he claims that a world view based on entropy (which can be equated with an ecological worldview) is beginning to gain momentum.

Given this implicit view of social structure and change, why does Rifkin offer no hope of avoiding collapse? The reason, I believe, lies outside his analytic structure, in the values he brings to the analysis. Rifkin's forecast of the future is actually a recast of the past. After the collapse of industrial society, after massive starvation and dislocation, survivors will eventually organize themselves in low entropy, solar energy based, agricultural communities. At first glance, Rifkin's vision may appear very pessimistic. In fact, however, it is the optimism of the Christian gleefully predicting man's ultimate fall due to his worldly ways. "Having banished God from society, the high entropy, materialist value system attempts to provide a heaven on earth" (Rifkin 1980, 204). Rifkin's damnation of industrial society is deeply rooted in his spiritual concerns. One gets the impression that he not only considers collapse inevitable, but right and just. After the collapse of the industrial infrastructure, after a considerable amount of suffering in atonement for our sins, a second Christian Reformation will begin. This reformation will lead man to both conserve the earth and share its fruits with his fellow man—a sort of second coming without Christ. While the collapse of industrial society can be extrapolated from present trends (assuming these trends continue unabated) of depletion and pollution, Rifkin's vision of the future has to be interpreted as a personal act of faith. The harsh environment of such a society, an environment that has been polluted and depleted beyond measure, would seem more amenable to a brutish existence rather than the high culture that is envisioned by Rifkin.

To fully evaluate the environmental challenge it is necessary to examine advocates of both sides of the debate who seriously address the concerns and positions of the opposing side. Such an exchange occurred between research groups working out of the Massachusetts Institute of Technology and Sussex Universities in the mid-1970s. There are some misunderstandings of both the MIT study and the subsequent debate in the literature. Social Problems texts, for example, often present a brief paragraph describing the MIT study followed by a statement that the Sussex research team had refuted MIT's "pessimistic predictions." But MIT made no predictions; they constructed a model (World 3) that simulated infrastructural and environmental relationships under a variety of assumptions regarding environmental limits, technological advance, and social change. Sussex did not refute the MIT study; they merely changed the assumptions of the model to reflect the technological worldview. The debate between Sussex and MIT is over which assumptions, which worldview, best fits real world processes.

The Structure and Dynamics of World 3

A system dynamics model consists of two types of variables: levels and rates. Level variables describe the condition of the system at any given point in time; rate variables represent change in these levels. By consulting the literature and experts in such fields as demography, agronomy, ecology, and nutrition, the MIT group first defined five components of the infrastructural-environmental relationship: population, industrial production, agricultural production, mineral depletion, and pollution. They then listed the causal relationships among the five sectors of the model and quantified these relationships in terms of levels and rates. The complex model they have devised is constructed along the following lines: (1) all five components of the model are interrelated; (2) growth in the levels of the five components tends to be exponential, this due to nature of population and production growth; and (3) there are physical limits to this growth.

All five components of the model are interconnected through a series of negative and positive feedback loops. In model simulations the level of population, industrial and agricultural production, depletion, and pollution are all governed by these positive and negative feedback loops. For example, population size is determined by the number

107

of births per year (average fertility) minus the number of deaths per year (average mortality). A rise in the average fertility rate will increase population size (positive feedback loop); a rise in the mortality rate will decrease population size (negative feedback loop). While the fertility and death rates depend on many demographic factors, such as average life expectancy and age composition of the population, these rates are also affected by conditions in other parts of the system. The death rate can be expected to rise as pollution increases, or fall if food per capita increases. Similarly, the birth rate will be affected by a rise in the standard of living. In turn, population size will affect other parts of the system. A growth in population will decrease the amount of food per capita, thus stimulating agricultural investment and production. Population growth will also affect the levels of industrial capital investment, depletion, and pollution. The World 3 model quantifies these interrelationships. It thereby simulates the behavior of the system by examining the impact of change of one part of the system on other components as well as on the overall system itself.

The quantification of this complex web of interrelationships is beyond the scope of this book (as well as this author). The World 3 model contains close to 150 equations relating 21 different levels contained in the five sectors. In addition, these equations contain numerous "clips" or shifts in the quantitative relationships between two variables. For example, a rise in the material standard of living will tend to increase the birth rate, but only to a point. After a certain level of the material standard of living is reached (estimated to be $500 per capita in the

World 3 model), the birth rate will decline, thus reflecting the demographic transition that takes place as a result of industrial development. Further, there are numerous delays built into the model that reflect real world processes. In the case of modeling the demographic transition, for example, it cannot be assumed that the social norm of family size is immediately reduced upon the attainment of $500 per capita of output; social norms change very slowly. Therefore, the modelers introduce a delay (in this case one of 20 years) between industrial output per capita and the social family size norm. There are approximately 21 delays built into the World 3 model, delays that reflect such real world processes as the appearance of pollution and its impact on mortality, or the technological and social response to the pollution problem. These delays serve to postpone the adjustment of the five sectors to changing conditions. The system delays are the main source of instability in the system.

Exponential Growth

Growth in the five components of the World 3 model tends to be exponential; that is, the level of each component increases by a constant percentage of the whole. The reason that the levels of all five components increase at an exponential rate is the interconnecting positive feedback loops between them. At base, however, exponential growth in the social system is rooted in the population and production sectors of the model.

> Population and productive capital are the motors of exponential growth in human society. Other entities, such as food production, resource use, and pollution, tend

to increase exponentially—not because they multiply themselves, but because they are driven by population and capital. There is no self-generation, no positive feedback loop, to cause pesticides in groundwater to create more pesticides, nor coal to breed underground and create more coal. The physical and biological consequences of growing 6 tons of wheat per hectare do not make it easier to grow 12 tons per hectare. At some point—when limits are reached—each doubling of food grown or minerals extracted is not easier but more difficult than the doubling before.

Therefore, insofar as food production and materials and energy use have been growing exponentially (which they have), they have been doing so not through their own structural capacity, but because the exponentially growing population and economy have been demanding more food and materials and energy and have been successful at producing them. Similarly, pollution and waste have been growing not because they have their own positive feedback structure, but because of the rising quantities of materials moved and energy used by the human economy (Meadows, Randers and Meadows, 769-778).

The factors that produce exponential growth can easily be seen with respect to population. An increase in the birthrate today would not only increase the present population but, after some delay to allow these babies to grow up and become parents themselves, increase the population of the future as well.

Industrial output also grows at an exponential rate. Again, the factors that account for this exponential growth are clearly discernible in the industrial sector. Growth in industrial output consists of both the production of consumer goods (cars, textiles, furniture) and capital goods (steel mills, factories, machinery). After some delay, these new capital goods are used to further increase industrial output. The exponential growth of population and production leads to the exponential growth in the exploitation of natural resources and the resulting pollution.

Exponential growth has the potential of being explosive. T. Robert Malthus (1798) gives and excellent example: "Taking the population of the world at any number, a thousand millions, for instance, the human species would increase in the ratio of—1, 2, 4, 8, 16, 32, 64, 128, 256, 512, etc. and subsistence as—1, 2, 3, 4, 5, 6, 7, 8, 9, 10, etc. In two centuries and a quarter, the population would be to the means of subsistence as 512 to 10: in three centuries as 4096 to 13, and in two thousand years the difference would be almost incalculable, though the produce in that time would have increased to an immense extent" (9). Of course Malthus was very much aware that such exponential growth could not go on indefinitely. The only reason for doing such a calculation was to demonstrate the power of exponential growth and the necessity to check such growth in a finite world. However, exponential growth combined with social system delays in responding to that growth may allow physical growth to continue beyond sustainable limits.

Of Models and Simulations

Models and theories are simple representations of complex realities. When dealing with complex ecological, climate, sociocultural, or cosmological systems the goal of the modeler is to focus upon the most important variables in the system and their interrelationships to one another. "To avoid creating impenetrable thickets of assumptions, modelers must discipline themselves. They cannot put into their models all they know; they have to put in only what is relevant for the purpose of the model. The art of modeling, like the arts of poetry or architecture or engineering or mapmaking, is to include just what is necessary to achieve the purpose, and no more. That is easy to say and hard to do" (Meadows, Randers and Meadows 2004, 2521-2524). The model does not reflect all the interrelationships of every variable in the infrastructure and environment—for such a mirror of reality would be as confusing as reality itself. Rather, the value of a model is judged on its parsimony and clarity of expression, as well as the accuracy of the symbolic reflection of reality that it creates. This accuracy can be judged only by comparing the behavior of the model to historical reality, something the World 3 modelers did when they ran their initial simulation in 1972 by running the model from 1900 to that date, and something that they also did in 2004 when comparing World 3 simulations from 1972 to 2000.

However, it must be emphasized that World 3 simulations do not predict the future; their utility lies in simulations of the interrelationships of infrastructural-environmental relationships under a variety of assumptions. The modelers can simulate changes in social practices (such as a change in the birth rate), new discoveries of raw materials that would significantly increase their availability, or the development of new technologies to control pollution. "We developed World3 to understand the broad sweep of the future—the possible modes, or behavior patterns, through which the human economy will interact with the carrying capacity of the planet over the coming century. How may the expanding global population and material economy interact with and adapt to the earth's limited carrying capacity over the coming decades?" (Meadows, Randers and Meadows 2004, 2526-2534). By modeling the most important aspects of the interface between sociocultural systems and the environment World 3 can simulate a variety of possible futures. But how sociocultural systems will actually adapt is beyond the scope of the model.

Environmental Limits

The MIT group maintains that there are physical limits to the exponential growth of population and production. In order to be sustained, infrastructural growth needs ever increasing amounts of food, raw materials, and energy. There are environmental limits to the amount of these resources that can be grown or extracted. The precise estimates of these limits are highly uncertain. Different social practices and technologies may allow the world system to grow more food per acre, or extract minerals from a lower grade of ore than is economically feasible today. In the initial simulation run, the estimates of limits are based on what the MIT group believes is possible given foreseeable changes in technologies and social practices. These estimates are then changed in subsequent simulations to examine the total system impact of new discoveries, technologies, and social practices that would affect these limits.

The amount of food that can be produced from the world's agricultural system is limited by the amount of land available for cultivation and the yield or output from that arable land. Recent studies indicate that there are, at most, about 3.2 billion hectares of land (7.86 billion acres) potentially suitable for agriculture on the earth. Approximately half of that land, the richest most accessible half, is under cultivation today. The remaining land will require immense capital inputs to reach, clear, irrigate, or fertilize before it is ready to produce food (Meadows 1972, 48).

There are several key assumptions of the agricultural subsystem of the World 3 model that need concern us here. First is the assumption that there is an upper limit on the amount of food that can be produced by the world's agricultural system. This upper limit is determined by the total amount of land suitable for cultivation (3.2 billion hectares) and land yield. The upper limit for land yield is assumed to be 10 times the inherent land fertility. The inherent land fertility "is defined as the weight of crops the land will produce in a traditional setting, using only traditional inputs such as human or animal energy and natural fertilizers such as manure" (Meadows 1974, 307). The inherent land fertility was estimated to be 600 vegetable-equivalent kilograms per hectare-year (the lower bound of most yield data they reviewed). Thus, it is assumed that the use of such modern agricultural inputs as pesticides, fertilizer, improved crop strains, and mechanization can increase land yield up to a factor of 10, or 6,000 vegetable-equivalent kilograms per hectare-year (about 3 times the global average yield in 1970). This limit is posited on a biological upper limit "to the efficiency with which the photosynthetic process can fix incoming solar energy into vegetable matter edible to man" (Meadows 1974, 297).

A second assumption of the agricultural subsystem is that of diminishing returns to investments in agricultural inputs and in the development of new lands for cultivation. The model assumes that development costs will increase as less convenient land comes under cultivation. While the model reflects the fact that increased agricultural inputs will increase land yield, it assumes that it will take increasing amounts of capital for each subsequent increase. These diminishing returns, according to MIT, are already apparent in the use of fertilizer, pesticides, new seeds, mechanization, and in the development of new lands.

While exponential growth in population requires ever greater amounts of food, growth in industrial production requires ever greater inputs of non-renewable natural resources. "Although the historical growth varies for each resource . . . exponential growth in resource production has been a general historical characteristic of the world economy" (Meadows 1974, 371). This growth in the consumption of nonrenewable resources has been caused by the exponential growth of both population and production. The authors go on to report that the U.S.

Bureau of Mines (1970) forecasts the aggregate world demand for nonrenewable resources will increase at an annual rate of 3.6 to 5.5 percent per year to the year 2000. Known reserves of natural resources such as coal, oil, copper, and zinc are measured in terms a "static resource index." This index attempts to capture the number of years that a particular resource will last at *present* consumption rates. For example, the MIT modelers report that the U.S. Bureau of Mines estimate that the known reserves of coal ($9.5 \times 10{:}12$ tons) will last about 3,100 years at present global production rates. If the hypothetical and speculative reserves are added ($7.3 \times 10{:}12$ tons) supplies will last about 5,100 years. However, growth in coal production is expected to average around 4.1 percent per year. If this rate of growth were to remain constant (it will not), it would exhaust the supply of coal in 118 (identified reserves) to 132 (identified plus hypothetical reserves) years. Growth rates in the production/consumption of other nonrenewable resources produce a similar pattern (although the static reserve index for many natural resources are much shorter).

The initial World 3 model assumes that the aggregate static resource index for nonrenewable resources to be at 250 years. This assumes that economically feasible substitutes will be available for those resources that have shorter static resource estimates (the liquification of coal to replace oil for example). Further, the model assumes that the cost of obtaining resources will rise as more resources are extracted from the earth. This is postulated on the assumption that the best grades and nearest locations are exploited first.

The further intensification of the infrastructure may also be limited by the amount of pollution the environment can absorb and recycle. Many pollutants are generated by the increasing rates of population and production (both industrial and agricultural), and the accumulated levels of pollutants around the globe are therefore rising exponentially. The precise limits of the earth in regard to pollution are not known. It is known, however, that many pollutants have a harmful effect on humans and the ecosystem when concentrated in local areas. The initial simulation therefore makes several assumptions. First, it is assumed that the environment can adequately recycle pollution up to 25 times the 1970 levels of pollution; after this level is reached, the expectation is that there will be a serious impairment in the environment's ability to assimilate pollution, and persistent pollutions will begin to accumulate. Second, it is assumed that an increase in the 1970 levels of pollution by a factor of 10 would have little impact on life expectancy; after this level is reached, however, life expectancy begins to decline at an increasing rate. An increase in the 1970 levels by a factor of 40 is expected to decrease life expectancy by 10 percent; an increase by a factor of 75 is expected to produce a 40 percent decline. A third assumption is that an increase in the 1970 levels of air pollution by a factor of 10 would have no effect on agricultural output; after this level is reached, land yields are expected to decline at an increasing rate. An increase in the 1970 levels by a factor of 20 is expected to reduce land yields by 30 percent; an increase by a factor of 30 by 55 percent.

World 3 Simulations

The growth rates of the five sectors of the World 3 model are completely derived from the complicated formulae that attempt to simulate the interrelationships between the various levels within the five sectors. How adequately these formulae reflect actual behavior of the world system can be determined by comparing the models' behavior over a period of time to historical data that are available. This is accomplished by setting the initial levels within all five sectors at their known 1900 levels (or estimates when these levels are not known) and comparing the simulated growth rates and levels to the actual rates and levels observed from 1900 to 1970. The model simulated growth in the world system closely parallels historically observed growth. While there were some discrepancies between the simulation model and the historical data available, these discrepancies tended to be small. The model, therefore, appeared to be highly reliable in reproducing the historical behavior of the interactions between the five sectors.

The World 3 model simulates growth in the world system by modeling the interactions between population, production, depletion, and pollution over a 200 year period (1900 to 2100). The initial 1972 model, or reference run, assumes that the numerical estimates of these interactions are correct; that the environmental limits of food production, resource depletion, and pollution are accurately estimated; and that there will be no qualitative change in our existing technology and social practices that would dramatically change the interactions or environmental limits.

"In Scenario 1 the society proceeds along a very traditional path as long as possible without major policy change. It traces the broad outline of history as we know it throughout the twentieth century. The output of food, industrial goods, and social services increases in response to obvious needs and subject to the availability of capital. There is no extraordinary effort, beyond what makes immediate economic sense, to abate pollution, conserve resources, or protect the land. This simulated world tries to bring all people through the demographic transition and into a prosperous industrial economy. The world in Scenario 1 acquires widespread health care and birth control as the service sector grows; it applies more agricultural inputs and gets higher yields as the agricultural sector grows; it emits more pollutants, demands more nonrenewable resources, and becomes capable of greater production as the industrial sector grows.

The population in Scenario 1 rises from 1.6 billion in the simulated year 1900 to 6 billion in the year 2000 and more than 7 billion by 2030. Total industrial output expands by a factor of almost 30 between 1900 and 2000 and then by 10 percent more by 2020 (Meadow, Randers and Meadows 2004, 3048-3057).

The model does well in simulating infrastructural-environmental relations historically (1900-1972) and in its simulation of future relations up to the year 2000.

Under these assumptions the model simulates a collapse in population and industrial production before the year 2100. In this run the collapse occurs because of nonrenewable resource depletion. The industrial capital

119

stock grows to a level that requires an enormous input of resources. In the very process of that growth, it depletes a large fraction of the estimated resource reserves available. As resource prices rise and mines are depleted, more and more capital must be used for obtaining resources in harder to reach places, leaving less to be invested for future growth. Finally investment cannot keep up with depreciation, and the industrial base collapses, taking with it the service and agricultural systems, which have become dependent on industrial inputs (such as fertilizers, pesticides, hospital laboratories, computers, and especially energy for mechanization). For a short time the situation is especially serious because population, with the delays inherent in the age structure and the process of social adjustment, keeps rising. Population finally decreases when the death rate is driven upward by lack of food and health services (Meadows 1972, 125).

At this point it should be re-emphasized that the value of the World 3 model does not lie in prediction but in simulation. The basic model simply reflects the best estimates of the interactions among the five sectors given our present level of knowledge about environmental limits and our existing social practices and technology. Because the model is explicit, numerical estimates of interrelationships and limits can be changed to reflect new knowledge or different assumptions; and these modifications can then be examined for their system interactions. It is by changing the basic assumptions that the World 3 model can be used to examine the impact of new technologies and social practices that can conceivably affect the system. Thus the model can be used to explore the interactions of the five sectors assuming a stable world population, or a leveling off of industrial production, or higher crop yields, or more efficient resource utilization, or improved pollution controls, or any combination of social practices and technologies that have the potential of changing the relationship of human societies to the environment.

The reference run assumes a 250-year static resource limit of nonrenewable resources. However, the modelers recognized that this is a highly uncertain estimate. New discoveries or more efficient utilization of these resources may extend this limit. Therefore, the research team also simulated the behavior of the world system using several more optimistic estimates as well. In one simulation they doubled their estimate of non-renewable resources to a static index of 500 years. "The overall behavior of the system is quite similar to that of the reference run except in three areas: industrial output per capita IOPC continues to grow 15 years longer . . . or until the year 2030. Population POP also continues to grow for an additional 15 years, reaching a level of over 8 billion in the year 2045. Pollution increases to 32 times its 1970 value in the year 2070, compared with the level of 11 times its 1970 value reached in 2035 in the reference run. Thus, after a 15 year postponement, growth is again halted by the effects of a decline in available resources—through a mechanism similar to that described in the reference run" (Meadows 1974, 504). The reason that a doubling of the static reserve index only buys the system 15 more years is that exponential growth of population and production are so explosive.

A tenfold increase in the static reserve index for nonrenewable resources, or from 250 years to 2500 years, effectively eliminates nonrenewable resources as a constraint to further infrastructural growth (at least within the time horizons of the model). However, under this assumption the model simulates a rise in pollution to intolerable levels, thus bringing about a decline in the system. While the exact parameters of the environmental limits are uncertain and open to attack, changes in these parameters can have little impact on the behavior of the model. More optimistic assumptions about physical limits in one sector of the model merely allow the system to grow until it is finally halted by another physical limit.

The reason for the collapse simulated by the World 3 model is not simply due to the specific environmental limitations, but rather to the dynamic qualities of the system as well. There are four basic properties of the system that must be addressed in any social strategy designed to avoid social collapse. These four properties are: "(1) relatively rapid physical growth, (2) physical limits to that growth, (3) possible erosion of those limits by overuse or misuse, and (4) delays in the feedback signals that limit growth" (Meadows 1974, 510). There are two basic social strategies for dealing with these system properties.

The first strategy, that of *Technological Fix* involves the uses of technology that attempt to overcome both the limits to growth and the further erosion of these limits. This strategy would include technologies that improve crop yields, promote more efficient use of nonrenewable resources, improve land management, and pollution control. The second set of strategies, that of *Ecological Fit*, involves social values and practices that address both infrastructural growth and the delays inherent in the feedback structure of the model. This strategy is an attempt to limit the growth of population and production before that growth overtaxes the environment. This goal can be achieved through long-range planning, social policies and technologies that limit physical growth, and promoting values that are consistent with environmental limits. MIT maintains that it is necessary to employ *both* strategies to avoid the collapse simulated by World 3.

Sussex Critique

There are several points of agreement between Sussex and MIT. There is complete agreement that many of the problems modeled by World 3 are urgent and of global concern. Both groups favor the development of national and international organizations for monitoring and preventing pollution hazards. Both view population growth as a serious problem (although Sussex sees it as mainly a Third World problem). Both groups also favor continued research and planning to avoid many resource and pollution problems. Finally, both groups are aware of many of the social ills associated with technological change. The major areas of disagreement between the two groups lie in their differing assessments of where these physical limits are and the potential of technological change to overcome these physical limits.

The Sussex critique of the World 3 model's treatment of natural resources is perhaps the strongest of their technical points. They first correctly identify the two key assumptions MIT makes about natural resources: "on aggregate, the world has 250 years' supply of minerals (at current consumption rates) and that the economic costs of exploiting the remaining deposits will increase significantly" (Cole 1973, 33). In regard to the first assumption, Sussex maintains that the 250 year limit is unnecessarily pessimistic. To ascertain the exact limits of the planet's mineral deposits two questions must first be addressed: What is in the earth? How much of it will prove to be exploitable by man? In answer to the first question, the Sussex group claims that mineral deposits are (almost) infinitely greater than assumed by the World 3 model. They maintain that much of the earth's surface has yet to be explored. Such exploration may yet uncover abundant conventional mineral deposits. Further, they point out that the earth's crust varies in thickness from 25 to 40 miles, and that the depth of present day mines is measured in hundreds of feet. Other unconventional sources of minerals include the core of the earth which contains iron-nickel deposits that are virtually inexhaustible, mineral deposits under the ocean floor, manganese nodules found on the seabed that contain a "wealth of minerals," as well as trace elements in seawater. All of these unconventional sources provide potentially exploitable resources. What limits there are come from man's economic, social, and technological ability to exploit them. In terms of man's sheer technological ability to exploit many of these resources, the Sussex group has not the slightest doubt. They point out that exploration, mining, and processing technology have all improved over the last century and that continued improvement can be expected. The only caveat to this optimistic forecast concerns the economic and social costs of developing and deploying these technologies. "The question has now ceased to involve geological reserves or even the potential of technology to exploit these reserves. It has become that of man's ability to develop such technologies, given what can be subsumed under the label 'economic and social constraints.' It is conceivable that the economic and social costs will prove unacceptable. The model assumes major increases in these costs" (Cole 1973, 40). The Sussex group maintains that it is just as valid to assume that technological improvements will continue to offset the costs of raw mineral extraction and processing.

The pollution subsystem of the World 3 model is criticized for lack of an empirical foundation and for aggregating different types of pollutants into a single index. According to Sussex, there is simply not enough known about the long term effects of pollution to warrant wide extrapolation. The assumptions regarding the production of pollutants are also attacked. "It is even possible to find data which support quite the opposite assumption to that made, namely that pollution can go down with increasing production" (Cole 1973, 86). This argument is based on improving technologies that can reduce the absolute levels of pollution while permitting increased production at minimal cost, and social value and political changes that force these technologies to be deployed.

This faith in the ability of technology to overcome the physical limits to growth, as well as the economic and social feasibility of developing and deploying these technologies, is also the central issue in the Sussex critique of the limit to food production. Sussex notes that, even with the "pessimistic" assumptions of the MIT group, there are still about 100 years of grace before an agricultural collapse. "This should give ample opportunity for very radical change, not only in plant and animal varieties, and in general husbandry, but also in the development of biological pest control, of direct methods of nitrogen fixation, of synthetic foods, of ocean farming and of food production on what is at present not considered to be arable land" (Cole 1973, 64). The Sussex group foresees continuing technological advance plus the rational use of the world's food producing resources as being sufficient to put off any global food crises. They do note, however, that there may be some political and social constraints in implementing these reforms.

Social-Political Change

The most sustained criticism that Sussex makes of the structure of the World 3 model is the charge that MIT has failed to incorporate the possibility of social value, political policy and technological changes into the model. Sussex charges that the MIT group has failed to incorporate social system constraints to further infrastructural growth. It is these types of constraints that many members of the Sussex group feel are far more relevant than physical limits. The incorporation of social limits to growth in the World 3 model "could only decrease the possibilities for growth allowed by physical limits" (Cole, et al. 1973, 228). Examples of this criticism include:

- "The MIT team tried to concentrate on physical limits to growth and omit changes in values, yet these changes may be the most important dynamic elements in the whole system" (Cole et al. 1973, 8).

- "The absence from the models of certain adaptive economic, technological and social feedback processes is considered to be particularly suspect" (Cole et al. 1973, 108).

- "Man is not pushed by a unified system mechanistically into intolerable conditions but assesses the circumstances around him and responds actively by adapting his goals and values whether in the intimacy of his sexual life, in the public sphere through the political process and economic adaptation, or in the change of customs and norms. Such adaptations occur as a persistent process when the strains of life are experienced. Man's fate is shaped not only by what happens to him but also by what he does, and he acts not just when faced with catastrophe but daily and continuously" (Cole, et al., 1973: 211).

The disagreement that Sussex has with MIT over the World 3 model's failure to incorporate political and social value changes is based on a fundamental misunderstanding of the purpose of the World 3 model. Sussex maintains that the failure to incorporate these political and value changes has led to an overly deterministic interpretation of man and society. There is certainly a good case to be made for

127

incorporating structural and superstructural feedback processes (both positive and negative) in any model of infrastructural growth. If the model were presented as a prediction of the future, this would be a devastating criticism. However, the World 3 model does not claim to be a prediction. It is a simulation of environmental - infrastructural relationships that can be run under assumptions of alternative social policies and values. While the standard run assumes no change in existing policies or values, subsequent runs simulate the behavior of infrastructural processes assuming the very policy and value changes that Sussex claims the model ignores.

While not incorporated in the formal model, they are included by changing basic assumptions in the model's parameters. For example, in one run they assume a stable level of population; in another, no growth in the consumption of resources (what the MIT team calls an "equilibrium state"). Further evidence that the potential of political and value changes are considered important by the MIT group is in the fact that they wrote their popular book. "Of course our purpose in publishing *Limits* was to encourage both the value change and the long-term planning process" (Cole 1973, 229). Because they interpret the basic World 3 model as a precise "prediction of doom," the Sussex group felt it important to point out that change in values, social policies, and technology may allow the sociocultural system to adjust to environmental constraints (thereby inadvertently arriving at the same conclusion as MIT). However, they place much greater emphasis than MIT on purely technological solutions to physical limits. In fact, when Sussex runs their own simulations on World

3 the only parameter changes they make are technological in nature.

It is difficult to evaluate their attempts at incorporating these parameter changes in the World 3 model. They are not well versed in system dynamics, making several elementary mistakes and being quite vague in their presentation. While they give some information on how they change the assumptions of the World 3 model—such as assuming that technology will be able to provide unlimited resources at a fixed cost while holding pollution down to about 10 percent of the levels assumed by MIT—they are not at all clear on how they changed the agricultural sector of the model. They do claim, however, that their simulations demonstrate that physical growth can go on for at least the next two centuries "on the assumption that, in the future, advances in technological, economic and sociopolitical activities will be made continually" (Cole 1973, 121). Presumably, the economic and sociopolitical activities refer to the economic opportunity and the political will to develop and deploy their posited technological improvements.

Technological Change

Sussex identifies the differing assessment of technology as being "at the heart of our differences" (Cole 1973, 10). They do not believe, however, that continuous technological development will inevitably occur. There are two perfectly respectable grounds for pessimism. It could be maintained on purely technical grounds that the world has now encountered or is about to encounter technological problems of such magnitudes that discontinuities may reasonably be expected. Or it could be maintained that, although technologically feasible, progress cannot be sustained for institutional reasons (Cole 1973, 11). They point out that there is some evidence of diminishing returns to investment in research and development. Further, there is evidence of a gross maldistribution of the world's scientific and technical resources going to military research. Sussex is also aware that political and other structural problems may delay the necessary technological response to many problems in resources and pollution. Finally, they express some disquiet about the feedback delays between the appearance of a problem, the social response, and the amelioration of the problem. Nevertheless, despite these caveats, the Sussex group is confident that by incorporating social and technological feedback mechanisms in the World 3 model, the "overshoot and collapse" mode of behavior can be avoided.

The differing assessment of the technical, social, and economic potential of technology to overcome physical limits is clearly apparent in the mineral resource sector of the World 3 model. The unconventional sources of raw materials discussed by Sussex fall into two categories: (1) resources in remote locations (i.e., deep in the earth's crust or under the sea); and (2) resources that exist in low grade, highly dispersed or high entropy form (trace elements in seawater, manganese nodules). Sussex believes that technological advance will enable society to economically exploit these resources. The MIT modelers, on the other hand, question the feasibility of exploiting these inaccessible and high entropy resources on both technological and economic grounds. MIT points out that the technologies to exploit and process the resources are not yet developed; nor is there any guarantee that they will be. More importantly, the economic feasibility of exploiting these resources is open to question. The fundamental postulate of the nonrenewable resource sector is that resources are present in finite supply and are distributed widely in grade and location. If it is assumed that the best grades and nearest locations are utilized first, then they will normally be used in an order of ascending cost, creating an identifiable "resource conversion path" (Meadows 1974, 382).

Basing their arguments on the physical laws of entropy and the hypothesis of diminishing returns on technological investment, the MIT group consistently questions the feasibility of purely technological solutions to environmental limits. In contrast, Sussex maintains that based on historical experience to date, technology can be expected to continue to overcome these physical limits— seemingly with minimal economic, social, or environmental costs. While rational arguments can be mounted on both sides of issue, the real difference is over an act of faith in technology.

While Sussex maintains that their "optimistic" assumptions about technology are just as tenable as MIT's "pessimistic" assumptions, their argument is weakened when considering the model as a whole. MIT makes this point in response to the Sussex critique: "We sought a framework in which many growth processes and limits could be considered together, to illustrate that conversations about superseding one limit are meaningless without considering the *system as a whole*. The Sussex analysis amply illustrates how easily any single resource, food, pollution, or population problem can be mentally 'solved' by assuming the sufficient capital, energy, labor, material, and time can be allocated to that one problem. Because they are holistic, the World models force one to explore the possibility that several of these problems may have to be solved simultaneously. We are interested in that possibility because our bias as modelers and our perceptions of exponential growth indicate to us that these problems will not come slowly, one at a time" (Cole 1973, 227 emphasis added). "Solving" the resource problem may well increase industrial production, thereby exacerbating pollution, which in turn could have impact on the agricultural subsystem. While the Sussex group does not completely ignore the structure of the World 3 model, the critique never adequately addresses the inter-linkages and long adaptive delays between the subsystems. The Sussex group points out that "continuous incremental improvements in various technologies have been tested in World 3 (by the MIT group) and not surprisingly the results are similar to those presented in this chapter" (Cole 1973, 133). What they fail to point out is that MIT characterized this simulation as highly unrealistic, completely ignoring real world processes. Successful advances in technology are by no means an automatic, continuous exponential process. They are subject to decreasing returns and increasing costs and to physical laws (for example, the second law of thermodynamics, which implies that recycling cannot be 100 percent effective or cost-free). Technological development is a delayed and costly process that occurs only in response to perceived social needs (Meadows 1974, 524).

"Technological policies alone can avoid collapse only if we assume that improved technologies can be achieved with no upper limit to their effectiveness, no delays in their development and deployment, and no physical costs in the system. If one believes that improved technologies can be achieved only with real physical costs and implementation delays, then the overshoot mode of the system still prevails . . . . Physical growth has not been checked, system delays still exist (and in fact new ones have been introduced), and physical limits to growth remain (Meadows, 1974: 537).

While substitutes, recycling, and conservation measures will buy time for industrial society, they cannot provide the raw materials needed for continued growth. While technological development *may* be able to tap lower grades of ore, even to the point of allowing man to exploit the trace elements in the seas, these technologies are by no means assured; they are likely to require huge inputs of energy and capital to develop and deploy, and they are still bound by the ultimate limits of the earth. Technologies such as improved crop strains, more efficient use of nonrenewable resources, improved land management, and pollution control are capable of extending the physical limits to growth, but we cannot expect these technologies to overcome environmental limits (technology, too, is subject to physical laws). Further, these new technologies not only have to be technically feasible, but economically feasible as well.

The World 3 model simulates the behavior of the system under assumptions of changes in social values (and thus structural changes) that reduce the intensification of the infrastructure. Specifically, the MIT group simulated the following strategies: (1) reduction of the desired completed family size to 2 children in 1975 (because of the age structure of the population, this would still cause a slow growth in population to about 5 billion people in 2040 before stabilizing), and (2) limiting industrial output to about 350 dollars per person year. This would be achieved by placing more emphasis on food and service outputs as well as an emphasis on the durability and quality of goods. While these social policy changes reduce infrastructural growth, they are not sufficient in avoiding a general system collapse. "To stabilize and sustain the model's population and industrial output, the social value changes that reduce the rates of growth of population and industrial output must be augmented by technological policies" (Meadows 1974, 543).

The MIT group points out that the type of technological and social policy changes they advocate can only be initiated as a result of long-range planning. It should also be noted (although MIT has not) that such changes could only be achieved through intense structural conflict; for limiting the growth of industrial output, promoting more efficient use of nonrenewable resources, improved land management, and pollution control are all long-term strategies with little short-term benefit to present structural hierarchies. Therefore, while the great environmental debate rages on, infrastructural growth continues its pace. Because of demographic reasons, population growth in the U.S. and many industrialized nations will continue for the next 30 years. Because of economic and demographic reason, population growth in developing nations will continue well into the next century. In 2011 the United Nations forecast that the world would reach the 7 billion mark in October of that year and 10 billion by 2100, though small changes in today's birth and death rates extrapolated over 90 years may produce huge changes. The impact of growing human numbers in developing countries have already degraded millions of acres of soil, destroyed millions of acres of rain forest and the thousands of species they harbor, and through deforestation, contributed to the greenhouse effect. But by far, the largest share of resources used, the largest amount of waste created is by the approximately one billion people living in industrial countries.

Industrial growth will not stop in the foreseeable future either. The dominant institutions in our society—both state and capital—are firmly committed to economic growth. As stated in previous chapters, the elite who control the dominant institutions in our society are inextricably committed to economic growth (a commitment they share with all governments throughout the world). Through these institutions people all over the world have become convinced that unrestrained economic growth is both necessary and desirable. Economic growth is promoted as our only hope of feeding and housing a growing world population, as well as the only way of improving our own standard of living. Within this consensus on the desirability of economic growth, corporate and governmental elites grow more powerful. Fundamental reform that challenges the existence of the elite simply cannot be granted. The present system is based on continued economic growth; it is essential to the continuation of the system itself. Stopping growth, or an equilibrium state as advocated by the MIT modelers, simply is not an option without prior social collapse and/or revolution.

In response to a deteriorating environment and demands for ever more consumer goods, industrial technology will become increasingly sophisticated and productive. What is workable (in terms of technical and economic feasibility) in nuclear fusion, synthetic fuels, superconductors, solar energy, mining of the oceans and the substitution of recyclable materials for those depleted will be developed and deployed. Pollution and depletion will increasingly be managed on a global scale. As the environmental crisis continues to intensify, governments and international organizations will act to limit pollution and depletion of the environment. However, the ecological principles employed in fashioning the industrial infrastructure will be the principles compatible with industrial growth and other interests of existing economic and governmental elites. Through the ruling classes the world is committed to economic growth; economic growth is endemic to modern industrial societies.

So, we are in a crap shoot. By committing ourselves to economic growth we are betting that technological development can be achieved that will tap into almost infinite supplies of energy and raw materials, with no delays in its development and deployment, at affordable prices, and with minimal physical costs to the environmental system. In order to offset the costs of depletion and pollution, our technology will have to become increasingly more complex and sophisticated. Technology will be called upon to tap into new energy sources, to go farther and deeper in our search for raw materials, and to restore parts of our environment that have already been destroyed.

In addition, these technologies will increasingly have to provide food, clothing, shelter and the industrial "good life" for over 80 percent of the world population presently living in developing nations. Further, these new technologies have the additional burden of providing ever increasing amounts of energy and raw materials to fuel an expansion of existing industrial states. This expansion is necessary to provide food, energy, and shelter to an expanding population as well as provide increasing material wealth to us and our descendants. Finally, this new technology will have to provide ever more efficient pollution control methods to compensate for the growth.

Personally, I place great faith in science and technology. I am aware of the potential benefits of the computer revolution, the pending biological revolution, as well as potential advances in agricultural science, new energy sources, and new sources of materials. Still, there are limits. Technological development may be able to forestall the "overshoot and collapse" mode for the foreseeable future, but it too is subject to physical limits. There is the very real possibility that, despite an expanding industrial economy, despite ever more sophisticated technology, general living standards will decline. In addition, given the history of industrialization and its effects on society, it is likely to cause further centralization and enlargement of corporate and government structures, and further disrupt traditional institutions and values.

Chapter 6: Post-industrial Dreams

But if we proceed without a thorough knowledge and accurate comprehension of the nature, extent, and magnitude of the difficulties we have to encounter, or if we unwisely direct our efforts towards an object in which we cannot hope for success, we shall not only exhaust our strength in fruitless exertions and remain at as great a distance as ever from the summit of our wishes, but we shall be perpetually crushed by the recoil of this rock of Sisyphus.

--T. Robert Malthus, 1798

When I wrote this book in 1992 the U.S. was still pretty much enthralled by theories of post-industrialism; the bloom is now off the rose and it is difficult to find a contemporary book that still touts the coming of a post-industrial society. Therefore this chapter is more for historical interest as well as a demonstration of how predicting the future can go so terribly awry when theory and history are ignored and simple trend analysis is used as your main forecasting tool.

Among futurists who take a more technological world view, the predominant image of the future is that of the "post-industrial society." Originally coined by Daniel Bell, the term is now generally used to refer to a future society based on a qualitatively different mode of production—a mode of production that has been variously described as based on service, information, or biological technology. While post-industrialists are in some confusion over the foundations of the post-industrial system, they are in apparent agreement that this new mode of production will greatly extend environmental limits through technology and the widespread adoption of new social practices that are less hostile to the environment than industrialism. It should be noted, however, that most post-industrialists rarely address environmental degradation directly; they seem to merely assume that these problems will be solved so that they can get on to the more serious business of forecasting the future.

Consistent with the technological world view, prophets of post-industrialism see technology as the solution to all of our most pressing problems. According to this view, not only will technology solve environmental problems, but many of the ills that have vexed society from the beginning of civilization will be eliminated. They see the possibilities of the new technologies becoming the foundation for a whole new social order.

According to some, information will become the dominant form of wealth. John Naisbitt (1982) in *Megatrends* points out that, since the 1950s, information occupations (defined as clerks and professionals) have increased from about 17 percent of the work force to more than 60 percent in the early 80s. This is the result, he argues, of a shift in the strategic resources of American society. In an industrial society, the key resource is capital; that is, capital can be used to create wealth. In the new information society the key resource is information; it is knowledge that now creates value and wealth. Because information can flow so freely through computer networks and because it can be acquired by almost anyone, it will not cause the kinds of stratification associated with traditional forms of property.

Such futurists forecast a time of decentralization, as political and economic decisions are increasingly handled on a local level. According to Naisbitt (1982), the federal government has largely become obsolete; state and local governments are fast becoming the most important political powers in America. The centralization of political power in America, Naisbitt argues, paralleled the industrialization process. Industrialism requires enormous centralization to coordinate labor, raw materials, and capital. The Great Depression ushered in an increased role of government into the economy. The two world wars and the need for full mobilization also caused centralized governments to grow. But conditions change. With the decline in manufacturing industry, decentralization has become the new organizational form in America.

The bulk of Naisbitt's decentralization argument rests on the decline in the power of the federal government and the consequent rise in power of state governments. Real political power, Naisbitt asserts, has shifted away from Congress and the executive to the state, cities, towns, and neighborhoods. Congress has become largely obsolete, and President Reagan (and one would imagine President Bush, Clinton, Bush, and Obama as well) was simply "riding the horse in the direction the horse is going" (10). States, on the other hand, are becoming more assertive. "During the 1970s, most states moved from two-year to four-year-term governors. State legislature replaced short sessions every other year with longer annual sessions" (104). Accordingly, states are becoming increasingly active in such areas as fighting organized crime, environmental protection, and building mass transit systems. In addition, states within a region are beginning to band together to further their mutual interests (for example, the Sunbelt and the Frostbelt). Businesses, according to Naisbitt, have also decentralized their operations. Increasingly corporations are locating major plants in rural areas. Decisions in these plants are often left to local managers and increasingly in the hands of the people who are directly affected by organizational decisions.

Participatory democracy, post-industrialists argue, will flower. Technology will allow people to vote directly on issues that concern them. According to Naisbitt, citizens, workers, and consumers are demanding and increasingly receiving a greater voice in the affairs of government and the corporations. The 1970s marked the beginning of the "participatory era" of political life, as indicated by the growth in the use of referenda and initiatives. Naisbitt writes that this marks a gradual shift in power away from elected representatives and appointed officials to the people themselves. While he does not predict the demise of representative democracy, he does predict that more and more of the serious issues that people care about will be dealt with directly by the voter through referenda and initiatives.

The demand for direct participation also extends to the economic areas of our lives. According to Naisbitt, consumerism is still alive and well in the 1980s. Consumers appear less militant only because they have stopped pressing for more government regulation. The new push will be toward direct representation on corporate boards. Other groups, such as workers, community leaders, and activist shareholders, will increasingly gain a voice in the running of corporate America. A final trend toward participatory democracy detailed by Naisbitt is workers' rights. The baby boom generation (people born roughly from 1946 to 1963) has invaded the work place with its "alien" values of individualism, its high education, and its rebellious attitude toward authority. Through sheer force of numbers they are forcing the corporations to recognize the rights of employees, including free speech, privacy, and due process in employee firing. Increasingly, Naisbitt argues, the trend in post-industrial societies is toward the involvement of people whose lives are affected in the decision making process.

Bureaucratic hierarchies, both Naisbitt and Alvin Toffler forecast, will crumble to be replaced by informal networks of people tied together in loose associations, sharing information and resources. There are several factors responsible for the decline of rigid hierarchical organization according to Naisbitt. First, hierarchies have proven inflexible in the information society. They tend to slow down the flow of information, just as greater speed and flexibility become needed. Second, we will move toward networking in response to Japanese competition. Workers in Japan, Naisbitt reports, meet together in small decentralized work groups; their decisions are listened to by people on top. Third, people are becoming increasingly dissatisfied with the impersonal nature of bureaucratic institutions. With the decline of primary groups in our society, such as the extended family, community, and church, people need to feel involved in their work. The typical bureaucratic hierarchy prevents this sort of identification. Fourth and finally, younger, more educated workers are filling the work place. Over 40 percent of the baby boom generation has a college education; there is simply not enough room for all of this college talent at the top. For all these reasons, Naisbitt claims, networks are the wave of the future.

In the decades after World War II, the United States dominated the world economy. In 1960, Naisbitt reports, the U.S. produced about 25 percent of the world's manufactured goods. Today, we have fallen to less than 17 percent. Japan, Naisbitt claims, is now the world's leading industrial power. It is simply too late to recapture the industrial lead. Other countries in the developing world, Naisbitt argues, with their supplies of cheap labor and abundant resource are much better equipped to provide high quality manufactured goods. In the new world economy, all countries of the world are growing increasingly interdependent. Yet our policies and goals as a society are still based on the assumption that we will continue to be the industrial leader.

As the developing world takes over major industrial tasks, the developed countries must "move beyond the industrial past, toward the great new enterprises of the future" (58). Some post-industrialists argue that we should let our "sunset industries," like steel and automobile manufacturing, rust. Instead, we should put our money into service industries and high tech "sunrise industries." These sunrise industries include electronics, biotechnology, robotics, alternative energy sources, and sea bed mining. Naisbitt recommends that government ease the structural readjustment by helping to retrain workers (government should supply the money; private industry can do the training) and promoting the growth of these "sunrise industries."

In terms of work, post-industrialists forecast the elimination of most boring jobs, the electronic cottage where much of our work can be done at home, increased leisure time, a higher educated work force, the elimination of environmental destruction, and increased opportunities for personal creativity. Robots will replace any remaining manufacturing jobs in the developed nations, they argue, most of the population would work in service industries, management, and high-tech industries.

Infrastructural Change

Are modern industrial societies undergoing a qualitative change to a new mode of production? According to most of these forecasters, post-industrialism is developing in our midst as industrialism is rapidly being transformed by the new technologies. The post-industrialists see these new technologies creating a new mode of production. Their case is seriously weakened, however, by their failure to offer any sort of coherent explanation as to what that new mode of production entails. The failure to even agree on a name (the term *post-industrialism* is simply a label that says what it is not) and the fact that the term *post-industrialism* has become a cliché in almost every graduation speech of the 1980s and 90s is some indication that the term is almost devoid of any real meaning.

Indeed, how have these new technologies changed our social-technological relationships to the environment? We still take our energy and material needs from the environment through extractive activities. We still practice agriculture with industrial machinery and the liberal use of oil. We still do the bulk of our manufacturing within the factory system. While they can demonstrate that new manufacturing technologies have taken us beyond the assembly line, their equation of traditional industrialism with labor intensive assembly line manufacture is flawed. Equating industrialism with assembly line manufacture is like equating physics with Newton. Nothing postulated by the post-industrialists represents a significant break with the industrial mode of production.

With an imperfect understanding of history, futurists posited an industrial society some 200 years old that was on the verge of transforming itself into a society based on something other than industrialism. In fact, while the industrial revolution is some 200 years old, industrial society—a society that is fully organized around industrialism—is a relatively recent phenomenon. Kumar (1978) argues that the first real industrial society did not appear until about 1900 when Britain had slightly less than half of its population involved in agriculture. It could even be argued that the first true industrial society did not occur until 1945 when America emerged from World War II. Since that time American institutions, values, and ideology have been undergoing rapid change to accommodate the needs of an intensifying industrial mode of production. Post-industrialists have mistaken this rapid change as the beginnings of a new type of society, when it can be more readily interpreted as industrialism itself. This postulate of a qualitatively different mode of production is essential to their forecasts, for it is through this qualitative break with the past that the post-industrialists are able to discount the tides of history.

The weakness of simple trend analysis devoid of theory and history is readily apparent in the predictions post-industrialists make about the occupational structure of their new society. They forecast a society based on the production of information and services. This future is predicated on the basis of several trends. The growth of the service economy in the 1950s was the first change of the occupational structure noted by the post-industrialists. In that decade the number of service jobs in the U.S. economy had actually passed the number of manufacturing jobs. Since that time, the service sector of American society has remained the dominant source of employment.

What futurists failed to note, however, was that the growth in service occupations has been a part of the industrialization process from the beginning. Service jobs have been growing at a faster rate than manufacturing jobs in the U.S. since the 1860s (Kumar, 1978). The growth of services in industrial society is related to the decline of the extended family and community as a provider of such services as child care, counseling, and social security. As industrialization continues to intensify, demands for geographical and social mobility will continue to weaken the extended family as well as the community and the basic nuclear family, thus putting even more demand on service industries. Services that used to be performed by virtue of family or personal ties are increasingly being performed by government or being integrated into the market economy. Not realizing that the service sector of the economy is an integral part of industrialization itself, many futurists seized upon the trend, extrapolated it into the future, and forecast a society based on service industries. Calling their vision a "service society," futurists failed to recognize the continuity of the present with the past. Identifying what they took to be a new trend, they extrapolated that trend into the future without any regard for system limits. Almost as bad, they misidentified the trend itself.

The tendency for futurists who write of the growing service economy is to focus on those services that are professional in character. They call forth images of lawyers and doctors and people doing managerial consulting. But the actual growth in the service sector of the economy has been far different. Unfortunately, the service occupations on the rise are the relatively low pay, low skill, low prestige service jobs—fast food workers, kitchen helpers, sales clerks, custodians, and nurses' aides and orderlies (Menosky, 1984)—precisely the unskilled occupations one would expect if government and the market economy were increasingly providing services to fill the void left by the decline in family and community.

A similar misunderstanding has occurred with the second occupational trend recognized by many futurists, the growth in high-tech information occupations. Menosky (1984) notes that proselytizers of computers claim that 30 million jobs in a broad range of fields will be "computer-related" in the 1990s. After examining the jobs, Menosky is not too impressed. "The '30 million' figure includes any job even distantly related to computer technology—from grocery store checkers using a bar code reader to retailers selling home video game cartridges. These people, comprising the overwhelming majority of the 30 million, will need no formal computer instruction to do their jobs" (Menosky 1984, 43). While the post-industrialists call forth images of computer scientists, programmers, and data processors, the reality is far different. Jobs that dominate the "information sector" are the traditional grunt jobs associated with bureaucracy—secretaries, clerks, and typists (Harris 1981). Again, these are the very jobs one would expect to grow as industrialism becomes more intensive and bureaucracies grow to provide the necessary coordination.

The post-industrialists are correct in asserting that America is rapidly undergoing a transition in employment from the production of manufactured goods to the production of services and information. But the purpose of a mode of production is to draw energy and raw materials out of the environment and convert it to human use. As the environment becomes depleted and polluted, industrial companies have to pay more for raw materials and pollution abatement. In order to maintain or increase existing profit levels, industrial companies attempt to reduce their wage component. Domestic capital flows overseas in search of cheaper labor (and no labor unions). Manufacturing jobs that remain are becoming increasingly automated. The whole point of technology is to apply it to traditional agriculture, mining, and manufacturing to make them more productive. The impact of the application of technology in these areas has always been to reduce the number of workers needed.

The manufacturing jobs being lost were among the highest paid working class occupations. They are being replaced by jobs that require minimal skills and education, jobs that offer little prestige, personal satisfaction, or income. Nor can the production jobs in high-tech (or sunrise industries) replace the loss of traditional manufacturing jobs. These jobs are not as well paying as manufacturing jobs in traditional industries. They are also subject to the same forces of automation and cheaper foreign labor as our traditional manufacturing jobs. Again, the post-industrialists miss the point of high-tech. It is a tool to be applied to government, traditional agricultural, manufacturing, information, and service industries to make them more productive; it is not an end in itself. In time that tool will be increasingly applied to the lower level service and information occupations as well. "As robots and computer software absorb an increasing share of factory and office tasks, the 'information society' will offer plenty of work for janitors, hospital orderlies, and fast-food helpers" (Winner 1984, 92).

The prediction that services and information will become the foundation of a post-industrial system appears to stem from a misunderstanding of the purpose of an economy. A mode of production can be defined as the technologies and social practices employed for taking energy and raw materials from the environment. Industrialism uses observation and science to fashion these technologies. Industrialism is a process; it is constantly employing science and new technologies in its quest for ever more efficient exploitation of its workers and of the natural environment. But society cannot live by high-tech alone. The point is to apply this technology to traditional extraction and manufacturing to make it more efficient.

Nor can we have a pure service economy. The rapid growth of services has been an integral part of industrialization from the beginning; it is folly to extrapolate this trend without its industrial base. We cannot all live by selling each other hamburgers, insurance, information, or managerial services.

Education

One of the chief reasons for the coming participatory democracy in both government and in the work place— according to the post-industrialists—are the high education requirements of post-industrial occupations. But while post-industrialists have been telling us that the information society will require an ever more skilled and educated work force, high-tech itself is having a very different effect. The application of computer technology to traditional industrial and service pursuits will not require a highly educated work force. High-tech will lower the overall skill level of the work force, not raise it (Menosky 1984). Technology appears to follow a skills curve.

As technology is applied to a job the skills required to perform that job tend to rise—job performance requires mastery of the old skills (say in the case of secretaries, typing, spelling, punctuation, grammar) as well as mastery of new skills (the use of complicated word-processing machines and programs). But then, as increasingly sophisticated technology is applied to the job, the technology becomes both easier to use and more efficient at performing secretarial tasks (spelling, filing, and so on). One need only think of the computer sophistication of the majority of computer users today compared to ten years ago—the machines and software are increasingly more "user friendly" and more powerful. The computer revolution has been a revolution of users not of computer jocks. The skills required of a user are minimal and becoming easier by the day. Some futurists recognize that low-skilled service and information occupations comprise the bulk of the new jobs being created in contemporary society, but they forecast that the further development of science and technology will eliminate the need for such workers, and professional and technical workers will soon predominate. Kumar (1978) labels the data to back up this trend as "sociological sleight of hand." By relying on the official statistics of the occupational census, researchers have failed "to ask what real degree of professional expertise, technical training, or education, might be involved in the increasingly common practice of assigning 'professional' or 'technical' status to a diverse range of occupations" (214-215). Kumar asks the question and finds that relabeling or re-grading suits the employees because it allows them to gain more status, and the employers because it is good for labor relations, but there is little change in the substance of the work itself. While he allows that there has been some increase in the "semi-professions," such as nursing, social work, and teaching, these professions do not enjoy the prestige, autonomy, or salaries of the traditional professions.

The majority of skilled technical and professional jobs in modern society do not require a highly knowledgeable work force in the traditional sense. Even the older professions (doctors, lawyers, scientists) are becoming highly specialized and increasingly employed by state or corporate bureaucracy—hierarchical organizations that tend to undermine the autonomy of the professional and routinize her performance. Education to attain these jobs has become increasingly narrow, focusing on technical competence as opposed to educating the whole person. While there is a traditional "liberal-arts" core left at most universities, it has been pared down to a bare minimum, and what remains has often been trivialized. At best, students look at the liberal arts in general education as something they have to get through in order to attain their desired job credentials. More typically perhaps, students look at general education as an empty academic exercise unconnected to the real world. The bulk of the jobs in a bureaucratic-industrial society do not require literate people with critical thinking skills. In fact, such people hinder the efficient operation of bureaucracies.

Jobs in bureaucratic-industrial societies are becoming highly specialized and circumscribed. Wendell Berry calls specialization the distinctive disease of modern character. "A system of specialization requires the abdication to specialists of various competences and responsibilities that were once personal and universal" (Berry 1977, 19). The specialist loses the competence to make decisions outside of her sphere of expertise. Americans now consign the problems of defense to the generals, problems of trade to the businessmen, problems of education to the educators, and foreign policy to the politicians. Within the work place we are restricted to our area of expertise; our job is to efficiently attain the goals of whatever organization we are working for. Bureaucracy and specialization release us from our responsibility to broader concerns. Neither community nor personal values are to play a role in our decision making. The individual loses both the competence and the authority to question the goals of the organization itself. Thus, a tobacco company executive can market his product to children; a car manufacturer can produce automobiles that explode when rear-ended; an industrialist can dump toxic wastes on empty lots. Without common bond and common values, community becomes impossible. A society dominated by bureaucracy does not produce the ideal democratic citizen. "People whose governing habit is the relinquishment of power, competence, and responsibility, and whose characteristic suffering is the anxiety of futility, make excellent spenders. They are ideal consumers. By inducing in them little panics of boredom, powerlessness, sexual failure, mortality, paranoia, they can be made to buy (or vote for) virtually anything that is 'attractively packaged'" (Berry, 1977: 24). The new technology simply makes the manipulation of people much easier.

Decentralization

Post-industrial dreams are founded upon an unrealistic faith in high technology and a serious misrepresentation of the impact that high tech is likely to have on our lives. The projected decentralization of power and control to be brought about by the "information society" does not appear to be happening. Relying heavily on the work of Winner (1984), it would appear that far from serving to decentralize power in an industrial society, computer and telecommunications technology actually aids bureaucratization and centralization. The primary beneficiaries of the use of large amounts of digitized information, Winner points out, are large business

154

corporations and vast public bureaucracies. As international competition for markets and resources becomes more intense, we can expect corporations to employ the new electronics to become more efficient and productive to meet the challenge.

Winner (1984) also forecasts that public bureaucracies will become larger, more complex, and more reliant on computer technology to tighten the coordination of the diverse activities within and between societies. Contrary to the assertions of post-industrialists, the process of centralization in America is already well underway. The horse that Reagan rode in the direction of reducing federal bureaucracy was on a merry-go-round, while he slowed the growth of federal power, he did not reverse it. "Current developments in the information age suggest an increase in power by those who already have a great deal of power, an enhanced centralization of control by those already prepared for control and an augmentation of wealth by the already wealthy" (92).

Winner claims that the key assumptions behind post-industrial dreams are seriously flawed. People do not face a serious shortage of information; rather, the shortage is one of education and basic intellectual skills to translate presently available information into effective action based on what one knows. Information is not knowledge. "While computers and information systems can increase the speed and flow of information, they do little to increase knowledge. Nor does knowledge automatically translate into power. Of course, knowledge employed in particular circumstances can help one act effectively and in that sense enhance one's power. A citrus farmer's knowledge of frost conditions enables him to take steps to fight the harmful effects of cold snaps on the crops. A candidate's knowledge of public opinion can be a powerful aid in an election campaign. But surely there is no automatic, positive link between knowledge and power, especially if that means power in a social or political sense. At times, knowledge brings merely an enlightened impotence or paralysis" (93). Post-industrial dreams are based on faulty assumptions equating information with knowledge, and knowledge with power.

Because the key assumptions are flawed, it also seems doubtful that the spread of information or personal computers will promote participatory democracy or greater equality in the workplace. The introduction of television did little to enhance the level of political debate in this country; in fact it has demonstrably contributed to growing voter apathy and manipulation. "The passive monitoring of electronic news and information allows citizens to feel involved, while releasing them from the desire to take an active part" (94).

Why should the computer be any different? The post-industrialists tell us that two-way interactive telecommunications systems will allow the ordinary citizen to directly participate in the political decision process. "But it could just as well lead to a serious weakening of individual rights, the destruction of many of the existing institutions of representative government and the gradual erosion of the confidence, independent judgments and leadership of public officials" (Burnham 1980, 240). While a two-way interactive system between the masses and their political (and economic) leaders is still in its infancy, the current popularity of instant public opinion polls gives some indication of how such a system will affect the political process. The present use of polling data by politicians inform them of what "bold stand" they can safely take (is my district pro-life or pro-choice?), what positions one has to lie about (the imposition of taxes), and what opinions one must pander to in order to have a political career (the sacred nature of the American flag). Particularly when combined with demographic data (which will be far easier to access in large data bases), these opinion polls also inform political operatives of the most effective advertising levers to pull to get voters to support their candidate or smear their opponent. At best, a two-way system will produce politicians adept at pandering to impulsive public opinion. At worst, it will provide further data to more efficiently manipulate the people.

Telecommunications and computers will also further centralize the power within bureaucracies. It is the large scale organization that has the capital and expertise to collect and manipulate the data; it is the large scale organization that determines what information is collected and who has access to it. While it is presumed by many post-industrialists that the widespread availability of personal computers will "equalize" the relationship between the individual and large organizations, it changes nothing. "In a contest of force against force, the larger, more sophisticated, better-equipped competitor usually has the upper hand. Hence, the availability of low-cost computing power may move the baseline that defines the electronic dimensions of social influence, but it does not necessarily alter the balance of power. Using a personal computer makes one no more powerful vis-a-vis, say, the U.S. National Security Agency than flying a hang glider establishes a person as a match for the U.S. Air Force (Winner 1984, 94-95). Burnham (1980, 14) makes much the same point: "Is it reasonable to believe that a dedicated band of environmentalists, sending electronic smoke signals to each other via their home terminals, really will be able to effectively match the concentrated power of a giant oil company or committed government agency?" Again, beliefs that post-industrialism will usher in a new age of decentralization, equality, and participatory democracy appear to be based on little more than dreams. Contrary to the expectations of post-industrialists, future society is likely to continue to be dominated by huge bureaucracies. The computer has been harnessed by large bureaucracies to increase efficiency. Bureaucratic efficiency, by definition, lies in hierarchical organization. Accordingly, the new technology has been conceived and implemented primarily as an instrument of managerial control (Howard 1985). Burnham (1980) ridicules the belief in the computer as the great equalizer in the workplace. "Can it really be argued that the personal computers and word processors now being purchased for more and more corporate employees and government officials will enhance their personal freedom? Or will the equipment, while increasing individual output, also allow a level of automated surveillance unknown to any previous age? Certainly the large airlines have spent hundreds of millions of dollars installing computer terminals to help their clerks sell tickets. But how many of the airlines are installing terminals in the homes of stockholders, or even of members of the board of governors, to give them more information about the internal operations of the company so they can exercise more effective control?" (14).

In manufacturing, computer systems have been designed to coordinate the flow of raw materials, machine time, labor, and other resources. With such systems in place, the front office can continuously monitor the production process, making decisions about inventory, manpower, and maintenance needs as problems occur. These same systems of control are increasingly being applied to monitoring clerical work within the organization. The computer is uniquely suited for this task as long as the assumption is made that the measurement of quality work can be quantified. Howard (1985) gives many examples of the constant monitoring of employees, including the following concerning Bell telephone operators. "Every fifteen minutes of the day, in Bell operator offices across the country, computer terminals near supervisor's desks print out the office's complete productivity record. In a ragged, staccato tempo, these Quarter-Hour Summaries list how many operators were on duty, how many calls they handled, the average 'speed of answer'--how long before an operator responds to the electronic beep of yet another incoming call. To get the productivity record of an individual employee is almost as easy. A supervisor merely keys the employee's number into the computer, and within seconds it prints out her performance for the day" (63). These records are then added to the ongoing record of the employee and the office. Continuous monitoring of worker performance is the logical extension of managerial control of the workplace. Both workers and line-managers can be judged by their performance.

The social science of coordinating and manipulating people within organizations has also advanced significantly in recent years. "Research into small groups, according to McGregor, showed that groups function best when everyone speaks his mind; when people listen as well as speak, when disagreements surface without causing 'obvious tensions'; when the 'chairman of the board' does not try to dominate his subordinates; and when decisions rest on consensus. These precepts which by this time had become the common coin of the social sciences, summarize the therapeutic view of authority. The growing acceptance of that view, at all levels of American society, makes it possible to preserve hierarchical forms of organization in the guise of 'participation.' It provides a society dominated by corporate elites with an anti-elitist ideology. . . . Therapeutic forms of social control, by softening or eliminating the adversary relation between subordinates and superiors, make it more and more difficult for citizens to defend themselves against the state or for workers to resist the demands of the corporation" (Lasch 1979, 314-315). By becoming paternalistic the system of authority is disguised; opposition to management becomes much more difficult to organize.

Bureaucracies are increasingly turning to the "human relations school" of management—using benefits, quality of work life projects, beer busts, pep rallies, stock options, and "worker participation"—to strengthen managerial authority. The object of the human relations school is to give the workers the illusion of control and a caring environment in order to engender loyalty and commitment to the organization. Howard (1985) characterizes the human relations school this way: "Let people feel in control without actually giving up your own power. Provide them with a pretense of participation in decisions that in fact are beyond their influence and control. Elicit the energy and engagement of close personal relationships, but make sure those relationships always remain contingent on 'usefulness' and performance. And don't ever become so close or committed to any particular relationship, any particular person, that it becomes an obstacle to exercising your authority (128). Under the human relations school, management becomes an elaborate manipulation of workers.

The new technologies and techniques much lauded by post-industrialists are technologies and techniques that enhance the efficiency and power of large bureaucracies. These technologies and techniques are harnessed by bureaucracies to more efficiently attain their instrumental goals. Whether the goal is profit, collecting taxes or intelligence, or getting elected, all else is subordinate to this bottom line.

Post industrialism became popular for a time because it provided ideological justification for corporations to move plants overseas for cheaper labor, lower taxes and lax environmental and worker safety laws. It served the interests of those in government who received the largesse of corporations to run their campaigns, or employ their lobbying influence after they retire. But it has become an increasingly tough sale in an age of rising inequality, middle class decline, and economic stagnation.

Chapter 7: Totalitarian Nightmares

History teaches that grave threats to liberty often come in times of urgency, when constitutional rights seem too extravagant to endure.

--Thurgood Marshall, (1908-1993)

The hypothesis examined in this chapter is that governments throughout the world are rapidly moving toward totalitarian control of social, political, and economic life. This is a very common theme among futurists as well as some of the more serious science fiction writers. But the hypothesis is complicated by the fact that there are two distinct visions of totalitarianism in futurist literature. The first is the type of authoritarian government that is based on terror and force. This is the totalitarianism that we are all familiar with: jackbooted police, intimidation, state controlled propaganda, and constant terrorizing of the population. The exemplars for such a system are Nazi Germany, Stalinist Russia, and the book, *1984*. The second vision can only be called the "new totalitarianism." This totalitarianism is founded upon the ever more sophisticated methods of manipulation and control given us by science (including social science) and technology. Through techniques of targeted propaganda, press management, surveillance, computerized records, and the rise of the therapeutic perspective—all accomplished within democratic and free market forms—the bureaucratic state exerts its power more efficiently than was possible in the past. This "softening" of power, placing the velvet glove over the iron fist of state corporate bureaucracy, makes it much more difficult to detect or oppose. The exemplar for such a system exists, many claim, in the United States today. Writers in the totalitarian tradition see control as made "necessary" by population growth, the increasing world competition for resources and markets (and subsequent calls for redistribution within and between countries), the increasing complexities of the industrial mode of production, and the crisis of environmental degradation.

Population

Today, world population stands at a little over 6 billion people. "Between 1980 and 2000 total world population grew from 4.4 billion to 6 billion. By 2015, at least another billion people will be added for a total of more than 7 billion…most of this growth has been, and will continue to be, in the developing world. In 1998, 85 percent of the world's people—more than 4 out of 5—lived in low- and middle-income countries; by 2015, it will be 6 out of 7" (World Bank 2012). The reason for the rapid growth population in the developing world is that such societies have experienced recent declines in their death rates (because of improvements in sanitation and health care) yet maintain a high birth rate because children are both productive assets and represent social security in old age. Because of their already large populations, particularly young people who are in their prime child bearing years,

164

the growth of population in the developing world is often explosive. The World Bank (2012) projects population will reach 7 billion in the developing countries by 2030, with another billion in the developed countries. Population in many developing countries is simply growing faster than their ability to produce food. These increased numbers are absorbing resources at an ever quickening pace.

The most apparent and widely publicized aspect of the population explosion in developing countries is the mass starvation and human suffering that results. A critical problem that has received much less attention, however, is the impact that this population growth is having on the social structures of these societies. In low-income countries more than a third of the population is under age 15. Because of recent birth rates, the dominant age category in these societies is 15 to 35. People within this age category are the ones most likely to be looking for work and housing. Youth in all societies tend to have high expectations. They are the young barbarians who have yet to buy into the present social structure. When their expectations fail to be met, they are the ones likely to rebel, engage in terrorist acts, or emigrate.

Developing nations are also increasingly urban. By 2008 more than half of the world's population, or 3.3 billion people, lived in urban areas. And this urban growth is expected to continue over the next few decades, particularly in the developing world. "By 2030, the towns and cities of the developing world will make up 81 per cent of urban humanity" (UNFPA 2007). Many of these people are being moved off the land by high rural density as well as mechanized agriculture (in an attempt to increase food production). They are also attracted to the cities because of the promise of jobs and housing. It is a promise that many developing nations cannot keep.

The people moving into cities are unprepared for life there. Lacking mechanical skills, often illiterate and steeped in rural traditions, they form a surplus of manpower without the skills necessary for employment. Worse, the cities are unprepared for them. Employment opportunities are simply not there. Developing nations do not have strong internal markets for industrial goods. The industrial products that they produce tend to be for overseas markets, their competitiveness rests on the exploitation of their workers and their environment.

Cities in the developing world are having difficulty providing for the basic human needs of their residents, let alone the surge of newcomers. The provision of water, food, sewage, and waste removal is hopelessly inadequate. "Rapid, unplanned and unsustainable patterns of urban development are making developing cities focal points for many emerging environment and health hazards" (WHO 2012). The ever growing concentration of people who are poor will intensify environmental problems such as pollution (solid waste disposal, sewage, air quality), and depletion (provision of safe water and food). Population growth in such cities will inevitably lead toward an intensifying the struggle for survival in these countries. The high concentration of people who are young, hungry, and unemployed will put enormous strain on existing political and economic institutions.

A tidal wave of human beings demanding food, shelter, work, livable environments, and human dignity may well engulf many developing nations. Aldous Huxley, in *Brave New World, Revisited* (1959), had this to say about the impact that population growth was likely to have on governments in the developing world: "In an underdeveloped and over-populated country, where four-fifths of the people get less than two thousand calories a day and one-fifth enjoys an adequate diet, can democratic institutions arise spontaneously? Or if they should be imposed from the outside or from above, can they possibly survive?" (14). Robert Heilbroner, in *The Human Prospect* (1980) writing of what he perceives to be the rather dim prospects for human life, forecast that this tidal wave of human beings will bring about totalitarian government in the Third World, believing only two outcomes are imaginable. "One is the descent of large populations of the underdeveloped world into a condition of steadily worsening social disorder, marked by shorter life expectancies, further stunting of physical and mental capabilities, political apathy intermingled with riots and pillaging when crops fail" (37-38). Heilbroner sees this type of society as being ruled by authoritarian elites serving the interests of a small economic and military upper class. Such elites would preside over the society "with mixed resignation, indifference, and despair" (38). Huxley (1959) provides the rationale for such a prediction:

> Whenever the economic life of a nation becomes precarious, the central government is forced to assume additional responsibilities for the general welfare. It must work out elaborate plans for dealing with a critical situation; it must impose ever greater

restrictions upon the activities of its subjects; and if, as is very likely, worsening economic conditions result in political unrest, or open rebellion, the central government must intervene to preserve public order and its own authority. More and more power is then concentrated in the hands of the executives and their bureaucratic managers. . . . Unrest and insecurity lead to more control by central governments and an increase of their power. In the absence of a constitutional tradition, this increased power will probably be exercised in a dictatorial fashion (10-11).

The rationale, it seems to me, is excellent. Beginning with Spencer many social scientists have pointed to the relationship between national crisis and increasing government regulation and control. In times of emergency, governments take on increased power. The probability of the forecast, it would appear, depends almost exclusively on the answer to the following question: How intractable is the population problem?

Since World War II, world governments and non-governmental agencies alike have pursued a strategy of "development." The goal of this strategy is to stimulate the economies in developing nations so that they can provide jobs for their citizens and, as societies, undergo a demographic transition. The demographic transition refers to the tendency of societies to stop population growth once a certain level of development has been reached. The transition is a result of a decline in birthrates, thought to occur because children in developed societies are no longer productive assets (with the passage of child labor laws and compulsory education) nor are they necessary as social security in old age (government and private pension plans take over this function). But the rate of population growth in most of these nations has outstripped economic growth and will continue to do so for the foreseeable future. Consequently, the task of developing the economy to the point of achieving the transition becomes more distant with each passing year. Worse still, the foreign debt of emerging and developing nations, much of it a result of ill-conceived development policies, is now more than six trillion dollars (IMF 2012). The debt of many countries is now simply too great to pay. Interest payments alone are likely to keep these nations in a position of poverty for years. As a result, many demographers are now giving up hope in the strategy of development. While we still pay lip service to the strategy, the world is not transferring wealth to the developing nations in any way near the amount necessary to implement the strategy. Rather, we seem to be pursuing a strategy of accommodation--giving aid to address the most visible suffering.

Heilbroner (1970/1980) goes a step further than Huxley in his forecast, positing a more "probable" alternative to the strategy of accommodation. Heilbroner foresaw the probability of "revolutionary" governments—that is authoritarian governments with dedicated leadership, extensive party structure, and an absence of inhibition in exercising power for the good of the society as a whole—to limit family size. Such a policy was begun in China in 1978. China's one-child policy was begun because the communist party of China recognized that the continued growth of the population would quickly eliminate any gains made in more efficient production processes. Even limiting the Chinese family to two children per couple would be a future disaster. The Chinese one-child policy consists of permission cards for having a child; block organizations (granny patrols) that visit women of child bearing ages to make sure that they are effectively practicing birth control; abortion; extensive propaganda campaigns; factory, neighborhood, and collective farm incentives for limiting births; organized social pressure on those who attempt to disobey the policy; as well as rewards and punishments to pressure families into following the policy. To date, the policy is having only limited success. The mechanisms for ensuring compliance have yet to be instituted throughout the country. In addition, the government has granted numerous exemptions to minority groups and rural farmers. If China's policy were to become a success, however, it could well serve as a model for other Third World nations.

The problem with such a policy, according to Heilbroner, is that such a revolutionary government would probably not limit itself to population control. A reorganization of agriculture, both technically and socially, the provision of employment by massive public works, and above all the resurrection of hope in a demoralized and apathetic people are logical next steps for any regime that is able to bring about social changes so fundamental as limitations in family size (38-39). Population pressures on developing countries will lead to the eventual rise of totalitarian governments, Heilbroner predicts, governments that attempt to control and regulate all forms of social, economic, and political activities.

Industrial Intensification

There are two very popular social-evolutionary ideas in the West. One is the idea of progress, dealt with throughout this book. The other is a tendency to view history as the unceasing march of man toward greater freedom from the constraints of the state. Aside from the frightening chord struck by George Orwell in *1984*, we almost take the march toward democracy for granted. With the bankruptcy of totalitarian regimes in Eastern Europe, our faith in the march of democracy and freedom has been strengthened. But Marvin Harris detects a very different evolutionary trend. "In anthropological perspective, the emergence of bourgeois parliamentary democracies in seventeenth and eighteenth-century Europe was a rare reversal of that descent from freedom to slavery which had been the main characteristic of the evolution of the state for 6,000 years" (Harris 1977, 264). Indeed, many futurists feel that democracy and freedom are threatened by the continuing intensification of the industrial mode of production.

One of the chief reasons given for the coming of totalitarianism is runaway industrial growth in both capitalist and communist countries. Here the hypothesis is that governments will be forced to grow in order to control the resulting depletion and pollution of the planet. "For it becomes increasingly clear that the central issue of the future will lodge in the capability of dealing with the environmental limitations that emerge ever more insistently as the most intransigent of the problems of the future" (Heilbroner 1980, 98). The regulatory function of

171

government will grow as it becomes increasingly necessary to prevent private concerns from not only polluting the environment, but from depleting strategic reserves as well. Government, the argument goes, must expand its economic regulatory functions to prevent economic growth hostile to the environment as it is the only institution in the position to regulate overall production processes.

Industrialism, under the auspices of capitalist economic systems, has been committed to growth. Economic growth serves two main functions for the social system. First, it dramatically increases the wealth of elites, thereby rewarding those who dominate the system. Second, economic growth provides a mechanism by which the income of the masses can be increased without seriously threatening existing distribution systems. There is no need for the government to play Robin Hood, taking from the rich to give to the poor; economic growth provides the necessary resources to keep the masses pacified. Growth is the mechanism by which industrial society increases the absolute income to all classes, leaving the relative shares undisturbed. Popularly known as the "trickle-down theory," it has been used repeatedly to justify tax cuts benefitting elites as well as government policies promoting economic growth and environmental degradation.

One reason for the pessimism regarding democracy is its past association with material progress. If material progress was to significantly slow down or come to a halt it is feared that the economic upheaval from below would exceed the capabilities of democracy to mediate the class conflict (Heilbroner 1980, 106). Without a growing economy to increase the income and living standards of the lower social classes, social tensions over redistribution are likely to explode. Heilbroner goes on to point out that in times of social crisis people often turn to centralized authority in the belief that it is better able to cope successfully than democratic structures. "As the histories of ancient and modern democracies illustrate, the pressure of political movements in times of war, civil commotion, or general anxiety pushes in the direction of authority, not away from it" (Heilbroner 1980, 128-129). This has been the American experience in terms of our Civil War, the two world wars, the Great Depression, and civil unrest throughout our history.

But a government bent on stopping environmental destruction, one that seriously limits growth of the manufacture of goods in the name of environmental necessity, would not serve the immediate interests of its people. Centralized government planning is not a viable substitute for free market economies in terms of meeting the biological and psychological needs of either the elites or the masses. Such a government would violate the central values of bureaucratic-industrial society, efficiency and the creation of ever more material wealth. As experience in the East has indicated, the hand of government on the rudder of the economy is a dead hand. Not only does government coordination of the economy place decision making in the hands of bureaucrats unfettered by either industry or market concerns, totalitarian government hinders the free exchange of ideas essential for technological and social innovation.

Moreover, such a government would be completely ineffective in stopping the environmental destruction perpetrated by other industrial nations.

The West, as well as the rest of the world, is committed to economic growth. Increasingly, this growth is seen to be fostered by free market economies and democratic governments. Social and technological measures to limit environmental destruction will only be taken if such measures are consistent with an intensifying economy. More drastic steps will be taken only if environmental problems actually reach the "crisis" stage; that is, pollution and depletion seriously undermine further efforts to intensify production processes. The World 3 modelers called this the "overshoot and collapse" stage.

Free market economies, unfortunately, are not suited to protecting our environment. However, they have produced an ideology that purports to minimize the problem—the further application of science and technology to extend environmental limits. Therefore, there is little probability that traditional totalitarian regimes will rise in the West to more "efficiently" manage the environmental degradation.

Heilbroner's projections are thus limited by his outmoded conception of totalitarianism. The ideology of democracy and freedom permeates the West; indeed the ideology appears to be headed for almost global acceptance. Any government system that evolves must encourage the continued development of science and technology—the old forms of totalitarianism do not. Any government system that evolves must efficiently coordinate and control extremely complex production and distribution systems—the old forms of totalitarianism have proven themselves incapable of doing so. Any system of government that evolves must have the hearts and minds of its people so as to efficiently coordinate and control massive populations—again, traditional totalitarianism has lost its legitimacy.

The New Totalitarianism

But there is another form of the hypothesis that is not so easily disposed. As environmental degradation continues, we will see the greater sophistication and complexity of production processes to offset depletion and pollution in order to maintain existing levels of production as well as provide for continued growth. These ever more sophisticated production techniques will require the further growth of huge private and public bureaucracies to coordinate and control these activities. These bureaucracies, consistent with the theories of Weber (as well as our experience over the last century), are incompatible with democracy. Increasing population and advancing technology have resulted in an increase in the number and complexity of organizations, an increase in the amount and power concentrated in the hands of officials and a corresponding decrease in the amount of control exercised by electors, coupled with a decrease in the public's regard for democratic procedures (Huxley 1959, 53-54). In accordance with sociocultural materialism, the intensification of infrastructure leads to the rationalization of social life.

The industrial mode of production exercises strong constraints on the organization of work, family, and even thought (Heilbroner 1980, 94). While industrialism can be defined as the ever greater application of science, logic, and reason to problems posed by our environment, bureaucratization can be seen as those same thought processes applied to problems of human organization. As the process of industrialization continues, the bureaucratization of structure and rationalization of superstructure continues apace. "During the past century the successive advances in technology have been accompanied by corresponding advances in organization. Complicated machinery has had to be matched by complicated social arrangements, designed to work as smoothly and efficiently as the new instruments of production" (Huxley 1959, 21). It is these new methods of social control that I call the "new totalitarianism." This new totalitarianism is not based on terror and external force, although the police powers of the state undergird its authority. Human organization that depends on the constant use of force and intimidation to discipline its members is extremely inefficient and ultimately ineffective. A system based solely on force must expend much energy policing its members; it stifles initiative, and it provides an obvious target for rallying opposition. The "inefficiency" of the old totalitarianism, its inability to fit in with the needs of an intensifying industrial system, is apparent in the disintegration of communist party power in Eastern Europe and the Soviet Union. Rather, the new totalitarianism is founded upon the ever more sophisticated methods of control given us by science (including social science) and technology. The truly efficient organization is based on the techniques and technologies of surveillance and manipulation.

Aldous Huxley, of *Brave New World* fame, saw this form of totalitarianism clearly. In his non-fiction work, *Brave New World, Revisited*, Huxley writes of the foundation of the new totalitarianism:

> In light of what we have recently learned about animal behavior in general, and human behavior in particular, it has become clear that control through the punishment of undesirable behavior is less effective, in the long run, than control through the reinforcement of desirable behavior by rewards, and that government through terror works on the whole less well than government through the non-violent manipulation of the environment and of the thoughts and feelings of individual men, women, and children . . . . Societies will continue to be controlled post-natally--by punishment, as in the past, and to an ever increasing extent by the more effective methods of reward and scientific manipulation (Huxley 1959, 3).

The scope and technology of monitoring and manipulation have grown tremendously since Huxley.

Surveillance

The use of sophisticated electronic "monitoring systems" is pervasive, even in supposed democratic societies. Video-cams are becoming commonplace—in stores, banks, subways, even on some street corners. It is possible to purchase sophisticated bugging equipment on the Internet. Computer information systems now have the capability of electronically monitoring most of our actions. Credit reports (and ratings) are instantly available on line to financial institutions and retail outlets. "Social transactions leave digitized footprints that afford opportunities that have a menacing aspect" (Winner 1984, 95). Employers and governments are quickly eroding our sense of privacy and replacing it with the pervasive feeling of being watched.

Other monitoring techniques include the polygraph (or lie detector), handwriting analysis, and drug tests (usually through the chemical analysis of urine). Until very recently an estimated 30 percent of America's largest corporations routinely used polygraph machines in screening job applicants or employees. Since Congress has prohibited such indiscriminant use, many corporations have turned to hand-writing analysis to uncover potential character flaws. "Long used in Europe by up to 88 percent of major firms, today over 12,000 U.S. companies, including Citibank, Merrill Lynch, Kodak and Farm Bureau, now utilize the services of handwriting experts …These are just three of over 200 handwriting experts in the country who advise both small and large businesses on their hires, based on what is revealed in the applicant's cursive script" (Edgerton 2012). The drug tests are one of the most recent threats to traditional guarantees against unreasonable searches and the right to privacy. Advocated by many government and industry leaders to combat the drug epidemic in America, many citizens feel the drug threat is so severe that the suspension of some individual rights are justified.

The threat of terrorism, especially since 9-11, has kicked surveillance of Americans up several notches with the passage of the Patriot Act. "Just six weeks after the September 11 attacks, a panicked Congress passed the 'USA/Patriot Act,' an overnight revision of the nation's surveillance laws that vastly expanded the government's authority to spy on its own citizens, while simultaneously reducing checks and balances on those powers like judicial oversight, public accountability, and the ability to challenge government searches in court" (Civil Liberties Union 2010). According to the ACLU "The Patriot Act increases the government's surveillance powers in four areas:

1.   Records searches. It expands the government's ability to look at records on an individual's activity being held by third parties. (Section 215)

2.   Secret searches. It expands the government's ability to search private property without notice to the owner. (Section 213)

3.   Intelligence searches. It expands a narrow exception to the Fourth Amendment that had been created for the collection of foreign intelligence information (Section 218).

4.   "Trap and trace" searches. It expands another Fourth Amendment exception for spying that collects "addressing" information about the origin and destination of communications, as opposed to the content (Section 214)."

The act allows authorities to access records held by doctors, libraries, Internet providers, and universities. This power is virtually unchecked; the government merely has to assert that the investigation is related to terrorism. The act also allows the government to enter homes and offices without the occupant being present; they can search, take photographs, and even seize property without telling the owner until well after the search. The Patriot Act also allows government to conduct physical searches and wiretaps on American citizens, again without providing probable cause as the American Constitution requires, all in the name of protecting our security.

The wedding of increased surveillance with computerized information storage systems is a civil libertarian's nightmare. Both public and private bureaucracies are growing in power. The growth in the power of both public and private bureaucracies in relation to the ordinary citizen, Burnham (1980) contends, is a direct result of their ability to collect, analyze, and distribute large quantities of digitized information. The new tools of the information age are employed by the old bureaucracies to further enhance their efficiency and thereby their power. "The computer thus has wrought a fundamental change in American life by encouraging the physical migration of information about the most minute details of our personal and public lives into the computerized files of a large and growing number of corporations, government bureaucracies, trade associations and other institutions" (Burnham 1980, 11). In the name of efficiency, private and public bureaucracies construct data bases containing information about our financial transactions, criminal records, taxes, credit, magazine subscriptions, employment, welfare assistance, health, banking, Internet searches and visited sites, purchases, and a host of other personal data about our lives. As a result, we have lost most of our privacy, opening ourselves to manipulation and control by these powerful organizations.

All of these data bases are built to make the organization more efficient in achieving its instrumental goals. For example, the Internal Revenue Service routinely uses the computer to detect taxpayer fraud. In one recent survey, 200 separate items were collected about each of the 50,000 individuals who had been randomly selected to represent the entire population of 93 million American taxpayers. "Once collected by the auditors, the 10 million bits of information collected by the survey were fed into a giant IRS computer for analysis. The result: a line-by-line, income-level-by-income-level, region-by-region list of probabilities that a taxpayer in any one of these categories incorrectly state the amount of tax due the government . . . .From the elaborate statistical tables developed from the periodic audits of selected taxpayers, the IRS develops its enforcement strategy for the entire nation, the marching orders for its 87,000 employees" (Burnham 1980, 109-110). "The U.S. government alone has collected more than 4 billion separate records about American citizens, about seventeen files for every man, woman and child in the country" (Burnham 1980, 51).

While Burnham writes about some abuses of these data systems (auditing taxes of Nixon's political opponents, the National Security Agency and other intelligence agencies tracking civil rights and anti-war demonstrators), it is the "legitimate" uses of these data bases that are far more frightening. Criminal records are routinely scrutinized, not only by agencies of the criminal justice system but by private corporations seeking information about their employees. Burnham details how computer programs have been used to match the information in many of these data bases. The Department of Health, Education, and Welfare matched the computerized files of federal employees to welfare recipients in order to detect fraud. Selective Service registration and student loans are now routinely matched; those failing to register are denied student loans. Tax rolls and other data bases are now routinely used to track down runaway parents and deny tax refunds, at first to those whose children have had to rely on public assistance to live, later to all those who avoid their child support payments.

The number and size of these vast data bases are growing, as bureaucracies seek to increase their power and efficiency. Electronic funds transfer systems (EFT) are designed to streamline banking; the systems will also allow increasingly detailed electronic monitoring of the individual's financial transactions and status. Marketers are currently experimenting with systems to correlate the buying habits of families with other aspects of their lifestyle. These same marketers are using similar methods to study the effectiveness of political messages and slogans. The problem with these instruments of efficiency is that they enhance the power of already powerful organizations over our lives. Because of their efficiency, we lose all privacy, giving large organizations the ability to use or abuse their data bases at will. "Computer scientists and manufacturers purport to believe their machines are neutral. This is true, of course, as long as the technology remains in the showroom. The neutrality evaporates, however, when powerful officials running powerful bureaucracies harness the computers to achieve their collective goals. Often both the goals and methods of achieving them are in the public interest. History tells us, however, that organizations of fallible men sometimes lose their way" (Burnham 1980, 84).

Even more dangerous is the danger of their further development and more sophisticated use. There is little difference between using computer and telecommunications technology to achieve efficient political administration and political domination; little difference between their use in efficient marketing and dictating to the marketplace. Virtually unchecked by law or custom, these techniques are the primary tools by which public and private bureaucracies increasingly dominate social, economic, and political life. "Unless preventative steps are taken, we may develop systems that contain a perpetual, pervasive but apparently benign surveillance. Confronted with omnipresent, all-seeing data banks, the populace may find passivity and compliance the safest route, avoiding activities that once comprised political liberty" (Winner 1984, 96). Even barring the centralization of these files for the foreseeable future, today both private and government organizations have unprecedented access to information about all aspects of the personal lives of the individuals they serve.

Manipulation

Tracking and matching individual records is not the only use of the computer to large organizations. The computer also increases the power of bureaucracies by providing them with the means of predicting opinions and activities of groups, thereby opening the members of these groups to targeted propaganda and appeals. Census data, magazine subscription lists, organizational and professional rolls, lists of political donors from the Federal Elections Commission are all used by organizations to predict political and social opinions of respondents and to tailor appeals for contributions and votes. These same and other lists are also used by major corporations to more efficiently market their goods and services.

Much of the technology of manipulation—radio, television, the printed word—was well-developed when Huxley was writing. Rather than inventing new media of manipulation, we have merely improved on the old forms and made them more pervasive. But advances in the techniques of manipulation have come from the social sciences as well as advertising. Focus group and survey information can uncover the emotional levers that will get us to buy a deodorant or a candidate, advertising through mass media can pull many of these levers at will. Campaign organizations, special interest groups, and advertisers can target their propaganda by obtaining mailing lists (from magazines, special interest organizations, or by matching zip codes with census information) composed of people likely to respond to the message. Governments manipulate the press through photo-ops and blatant propaganda so often that it is not even news anymore—the American people, if they recognize it at all, seem to accept it as normal behavior by their government officials. Press agents and "spin doctors" put the best face on disasters. Image, particularly the image put forth on television, has become more important than reality.

It was Huxley's belief that impersonal social forces, such as environmental depletion brought on by runaway population and industrial growth, were pushing democracies toward the necessity of more efficiently coordinating its population. The growth of formal organizations as well as advances in the science and technology of manipulation were meeting this need for control. The drift toward totalitarianism was being accelerated, he believed, by the self-interest of elites at the top of commercial and political hierarchies. Commercial propaganda is essential in a capitalistic society. The techniques of advertising rely on the manipulation of symbols that attempt to create a bridge between the consumer's unconscious desires, fears, or anxieties and the product being sold. The objective of advertising is to get the consumer to believe that the purchase of the product will make his dream come true, or that she will be able to avoid her worst fears. But the advertising techniques developed to sell industrial goods and services are harmful when applied to political campaigns. Democracy can only survive if the people stay knowledgeable and make rational choices based on unbiased information and enlightened self- interest. "A dictatorship, on the other hand, maintains itself by censoring or distorting the facts, and by appealing, not to reason, not to enlightened self-interest, but to passion and prejudice, to the powerful 'hidden forces,' as Hitler called them, present in the unconscious depths of every human mind" (Huxley 1959, 45). Democratic institutions, Huxley believed, were increasingly being undermined from within by politicians and their propagandists.

In one particularly prophetic passage, Huxley writes of the candidate of the future: "In one way or another, as vigorous he-man or kindly father, the candidate must be glamorous. He must also be an entertainer who never bores his audience. Inured to television and radio, that audience is accustomed to being distracted and does not like to be asked to concentrate or make a prolonged intellectual effort. All speeches of the entertainer-candidate must therefore be short and snappy. The great issues of the day must be dealt with in five minutes at the most—and preferable (since the audience will be eager to pass on to something a little livelier than inflation or the H-bomb) in sixty seconds flat" (Huxley 1959, 55). Political propagandists and their candidates make no attempt to educate people for self-government; they are content to merely exploit them for their votes. While the present day corruption of the political campaign is widely recognized, it is usually perceived as only a slight problem in democratic procedures, in need of reform but certainly nothing that threatens the foundation of the system. After all, it is reasoned, 'trivial' campaigns are well known in American history. Such a view ignores the present day sophistication and pervasiveness of manipulative technology; it also ignores the increasing role of money in political the political discourse.

Huxley sees the "quaint old forms" and trappings of democracy—elections, supreme courts, congress, the constitution—as remaining in place. The traditional names and slogans will remain; freedom and democracy will continue to be the theme of presidential speeches and editorials. As in the present day, political scientists and sociologists will continue to be in hot debate over the Power Elitist hypothesis. But it will be democracy and freedom in a trivial sense. "Meanwhile the ruling oligarchy and its highly trained elite of soldiers, policemen, thought manufacturers and mind-manipulators will quietly run the show as they see fit" (Huxley 1959, 108).

The belief in democracy actually works to the advantage of the power elite, as Parenti (1978) has noted in the following passage:

> As now constituted, elections serve as a great asset in consolidating the existing social order by propagating the appearances of popular rule. History demonstrates that the people might be moved to overthrow a tyrant who shows himself provocatively indifferent to their woes, but they are far less inclined to make war upon a state, even one dominated by the propertied class, if it preserves what Madison called 'the spirit and form of popular government.' Elections legitimate the rule of the propertied class by investing it with the moral authority of popular consent. By the magic of the ballot, class dominance becomes 'democratic' governance. According to the classical theory of democracy, the purpose of

suffrage is to make the rulers more responsive to the will of the people. But history suggests the contrary: more often the effect and even the intent of suffrage has been to make the enfranchised group more responsive to the rulers, or at least committed to the ongoing system of rule. In the classical theory, the vote is an exercise of sovereign power, a popular command over the rulers, but it might just as easily be thought of as an act of support extended by the electorate to those above them. Hence, an election is more a surrender than an assertion of popular power, a gathering up of empowering responses by the elites who have the resources for such periodic harvestings, an institutionalized mechanism providing for the regulated flow of power from the many to the few in order to legitimate the rule of the few in the name of the many (201).

Once in office, the campaign tactics of manipulation will carry over into styles of governance. "Therapy" for the deviant and the criminal all in the name of scientific advance and enlightenment will become more the norm. Basing its perspective on the medical model of care, the therapeutic solution to the problem of social control is focused on changing the individual to better fit the social environment. It purports to treat the "causes" of crime and deviance instead of merely dealing with its consequences. Under the therapeutic perspective, crime and deviance become diseases, to be treated with chemo- or psychotherapy. People diverted from the criminal justice system and placed under this medical model of treatment are denied basic constitutional safeguards. Consequently, under such a system, the coercive power of the state increases dramatically. Such reforms are difficult to oppose because they seem to be the epitome of enlightenment.

The state, rather than acting as an agent of punishment, is acting as a "friend" and "helper." But by doing so it is denying the political nature of the deviant act; it is removing an impetus to improve social conditions. The last ditch effort at controlling crime and deviance is but the most obvious form of manipulation. In the name of welfare, the environment, child abuse prevention, social security, nationalized medical care, to name but a few of the laudable goals, state power will confront the individual everywhere. As the science and technique of manipulation continue to improve and become more pervasive, the *Brave New World* nightmare becomes more of a reality.

Chapter 8: The Evolution of the Future

To this day there has never existed a bureaucracy which could compare with that of Egypt. This is known to everyone who knows the social history of ancient times; and it is equally apparent that to-day we are proceeding towards an evolution which resembles that system in every detail, except that it is built on other foundations, on technically more perfect, more rationalized, and therefore much more mechanized foundations. The problem which beset us now is not: how can this evolution be changed?—for that is impossible, but what will come of it?

--Max Weber, 1909

Books of this sort, commonly called "gloom and doom" in the literature, typically offer some last minute ray of hope in the concluding chapter. Something of the sort that claims that if we act now to change current trends we can avoid our fate. But these projections are made on the basis of systems theory, elite interests, as well as my understandings of the history of social evolution in the West. Short of a world-wide social revolution, this leads me to the conclusion that further infrastructural intensification is inevitable, both to offset depletion and pollution and to provide the material wealth for the "good life" to at least a portion of the population. All else necessarily follows.

Adopting a systems view of society and nature means that one is sensitive to the fact that all of the parts of the social system fit together. All of the components of society—economic institutions, government, family, values, and norms—are interrelated. This means that a change of any part of the social web will inevitably have ramifications on other parts of the social system. And this insight leads to a very sobering conclusion: "We can never do merely one thing." All industrial nations on earth are attempting to do *one* thing, they are expanding their industrial infrastructures. So the question becomes what impact will economic growth have on the rest of the sociocultural system? In this final chapter I would like to briefly summarize the impact that further industrial intensification is likely to have on our natural environment; on institutional structures such as family, community, government, and corporations; and finally on individual personality.

Infrastructural Intensification

Infrastructural growth can be expected to push up against environmental limits of non-renewable resources, renewable resources, and pollution within the foreseeable future. World shortages of energy and raw materials as well as pollution were the theme of the *Global 2000 Report to the President*. Commissioned by Jimmy Carter and issued in 1980 (and promptly ignored by the Reagan administration), the 2000 report used projections from 11 separate federal agencies. The report concluded: "If present trends continue, the world in 2000 will be more crowded, more polluted, less stable ecologically, and more vulnerable to disruption than the world we live in now" (Barney, 1980). The federal government projects more people, more poor, a wider gap between rich and poor nations, greater income disparities within countries, less

192

arable land, less petroleum reserve, less water, less growing stock of wood, higher atmospheric concentrations of carbon dioxide (the greenhouse gas), increasing desertification, higher prices (over and above inflation), and greater dependence of most nations on foreign sources of energy.

They offer one caveat. They feel their report may be too optimistic. This is because there was little coordination between the federal agencies. Thus, the Departments of Agriculture, Urban Affairs, and Energy all used the same sources for solving impending shortages of water; all assumed remaining resources would be available to solve shortages in their particular area. Other agencies tapped into the same reserves of oil, natural gas and coal. They failed to look at environmental problems in terms of their systemic nature. Even on the basis of their optimistic projections, however, the immediate future looks pretty bleak.

They conclude their report with the following statement: "For hundreds of millions of desperately poor, the outlook for food and other necessities of life will be no better. For many it will be worse. Barring revolutionary advances in technology, life for most people on earth will be more precarious in 2000 than it is now—unless the nations of the world act decisively to alter the current trends" (Barney, 1980). The nations of the world have yet to act decisively; instead we have put our faith in technology. The only ecological principles that are integrated into the industrial production processes are those that do not directly threaten industrial growth.

Primary Groups

193

As industrialization continues to intensify, primary groups such as the family and community will continue to lose many of their functions. This decline in the influence of primary groups has the potential of radically altering social life. Perhaps the greatest change in modern society in the last thirty years has been the shift in employment of married women from domestic and child-care services within the home to employment in the market economy. In large part, this shift in employment has been caused by an attempt to maintain middle class living standards in the modern economy (Harris 1981). A further factor behind the employment of women outside the home has been the growth of bureaucratic and service jobs caused by industrial intensification (Harris 1981). At first, industrial intensification weakened the extended family system. Emphasis on the nuclear family unit was essential for social and geographical mobility. Now, with both husband and wife working outside the home, this mobility is increasingly important for each. Further industrial intensification puts the nuclear family itself at risk.

One impact of industrialization on the family is smaller family size. As the state forbids child labor outside the home and increasingly provides economic security in old age, there are fewer reasons to have children. In an advanced industrial society in which married women are increasingly being employed outside the home and the cost of raising a child is a major financial commitment (and material wealth is a major value) there are even fewer reasons. Having no or few children makes the marriage bond less stable.

Beyond marriage, there are other social implications. Consider the "one child" policy of China. If the Chinese one child policy were to become a success, it would have dramatic impact on the future of family life in China. Since the Chinese, like most cultures, highly value males, female infanticide has again become a problem. If this were to continue, extreme imbalances in the male/female ratio would result—with many ramifications for the rest of Chinese culture. In addition, a one child policy consistently followed for more than a generation would mean that families would consist of little more than the nuclear unit—children would have no siblings, aunts or uncles, or close cousins. The Chinese family unit would consist of a child, aging parents and grandparents. Such a policy would rapidly undermine the power and influence of primary groups in society, causing an even more rapid acceleration in the growth of secondary service organizations. Socialization will increasingly take place within secondary organizations. As married women continue to work outside the home, day care, pre-school, and after-school care will continue to proliferate. Socialization in secondary organizations at such an early age (infants of two weeks are not uncommon) teaches the child to "live" within bureaucratic structures. This increasing rationalization of the socialization process will speed social change, as well as expose our youth at an increasingly earlier age to the direct influence of elite ideas and ideologies. In the past, family and community influence on childhood socialization acted as a brake on rapid social change. For example, intellectuals, churches, and schools could preach tolerance and acceptance of different races, but the family preaching racism had a more direct and lasting influence on the formation of the child's personality. With the advent of day care, the balance began to change. These secondary organizations, organized along rational lines and subject to government regulation and inspection, socialize the child in accordance with the "latest" social mores and conventions. Mass media programming aimed at children, children's books and movies hammer in the same message. While the child may be exposed to conflicting messages from family and later peers, the influence of these more traditional agents of socialization is waning.

Secondary Organization

America and other industrial nations of the world are rapidly undergoing a transition in employment from the production of goods to the production of services and information. There are several reasons for this trend. The whole point of technology is to apply it to traditional agriculture and manufacturing to make them more "efficient" and productive. The impact of the application of high tech in these areas will be to reduce the number of workers needed. Domestic capital is flowing overseas at an increasing rate in search of cheap labor (and more lax environmental and occupational safety laws). Production jobs that remain in advanced industrial societies are increasingly becoming automated as industrial companies attempt to reduce their wage component in order to maintain or increase existing profit levels.

As industrialization continues to intensify, demands for geographical and social mobility will continue to weaken the extended family as well as the basic nuclear family, thus putting even more demand on service industries. Services that used to be performed by virtue of family ties are increasingly being performed by government or being integrated into the market economy. Most of these service jobs are relatively low pay, low skill occupations such as kitchen helpers, custodians, and nurses' aides and orderlies.

The bulk of the much vaunted "information" occupations of the post-industrialists are the white-collar, low-level bureaucratic jobs of old. As industrial technologies become more complex and require ever greater inputs of capital to purchase and operate, corporations become larger, and the need for bureaucracy to coordinate and control these far-flung empires becomes more acute. As international competition becomes more intense, we can expect corporations to become larger to meet the challenges.

The application of high tech to these information and service occupations is lowering the overall skill levels of the work force, making these people poorer and less educated. The new wave of automation presently sweeping through traditional bureaucracies and service organizations is done in the name of efficiency. Electronic work stations and the like are not only more efficient in performing work tasks; they are also ideal for monitoring employee performance. They offer the hope to the corporate manager of controlling the most unpredictable part of the work process—human performance.

Recent structural changes made in response to the intensifying infrastructure also point toward increasing totalitarian control through bureaucratization and the resulting oligarchy. Government and corporate growth in the twentieth century has been phenomenal. Whatever the outcome of the environmental crisis, whether the process results in environmental collapse or technological innovations that "overcome" environmental constraints, government and corporations will increase their power to deal with the crisis. In the name of welfare, efficiency, environment, taxation, and education, to name but a few of the laudable goals, government has expanded and will continue to expand its power and influence. The prospects for real democracy in such a society are dismal.

Huxley sees the rise of a new totalitarianism based on manipulation rather than terror. "In the more efficient dictatorships of tomorrow there will probably be much less violence than under Hitler and Stalin. The future dictator's subjects will be painlessly regimented by a corps of highly trained social engineers" (Huxley 1959, 25). Modern technology and techniques have led to a concentration of economic and political power in huge bureaucracies that increasingly control social life. This control is hidden, manipulative, and almost inconspicuous; and thus it is extremely efficient and effective.

Rationalization of Superstructure

According to C. Wright Mills, the most important question to ask of society is 'What kinds of men and women does it tend to create? What personal styles of life does it inculcate and reinforce?' (Mills 1959). Asking this question with respect to the future society sketched out in these pages is not reassuring. Increasingly our lives are being spent in rational secondary organizations designed to perform like machines. These hierarchical organizations are dominated by the goals and "values" of economic elites. The efficient operation of these organizations depends upon the workers' ability to perform the narrow specialized role assigned to maximize organizational efficiency. Clients of the organization (or patients, or customers, or students) are likewise dehumanized, treated as categories based on status rather than as human beings. A society increasingly dominated by such organizations, one that socializes its children into these organizations at an increasingly earlier age, is a society that is redefining what it means to be human.

Many social critics have identified the failure of modern industrial society to provide meaningful roles to individuals as one of its greatest failures. Modern society replaces religion with science, tradition with pragmatism, mystery with predictability, and universal values with "efficiency." It is argued that there are limits to the decline of primary groups in social life, limits on the extent to which we can cut ourselves off from our humanity by performing our narrow, specialized roles within organizational structures. These natural human limits, it is argued, will prevent modern bureaucratic-industrial societies from rationalizing much further. Marx even predicted the evolution of a more humane society based partly on humanity's reaction against dehumanization. I suspect, however, that these natural limits are not part of human nature, but rather are learned.

Modern industrial society is indeed alien to those raised in a more traditional culture. Such individuals serve to slow down the rationalization process, rebelling, stalling, subverting, adulterating human machines with "outdated" values and traditions. Sometimes they even manage to socialize members of the next generation into accepting their "quaint" values and perspectives (although, with the impact of new and more powerful agencies of socialization, this is becoming rare). Rationalization is a process, however, and each succeeding generation extends its limits.

Huxley saw no natural human limit to the rationalization process. "In their original form human societies bore no resemblance to the hive or the ant heap; they were merely packs. Civilization is, among other things, the process by which primitive packs are transformed into an analogue, crude and mechanical, of the social insects' organic communities. At the present time the pressures of over population and technological change are accelerating this process" (Huxley 1959, 22). Industrialism is intensifying. From the beginning, industrialism has used science and technology to offset the effects of depletion and pollution. It will continue to do so, though whether it can be done indefinitely is arguable. From the beginning industrialism has furthered the trends of centralization and bureaucratization, causing the growth of the power and control of formal organizations over our lives as well as placing unprecedented power and control in the hands of the elites at the top of these organizations. Computers and telecommunications systems, as well as other forms of high technology will simply accelerate this process. From the beginning industrialism has weakened primary groups such as the family and community. All indications are that this trend is continuing. From the beginning industrialism has eroded religious and spiritual values, as well as traditions that are in conflict with an ever intensifying infrastructure. Again, there appears to be no significant reversal of this trend. Therefore, in our considerations of the future, we must expect a great deal of continuity with our past.

2012 Addendum

As I said in the introduction, I think my 1991 analysis and conclusions hold up well. If I were to completely rewrite the book I would give more attention to the role of capitalism in social evolution. Since 1991 I have developed far more appreciation for Karl Marx's subtle analysis of the contradictions of capital (though little for his proposed solution of socialism). Corporate influence over the agenda, parameters of debate, and actions of governments has certainly become far more overt in America. The war machine continues almost unchallenged. Obama's modest attempts at reform of other parts of the system are resisted tooth and nail even by elements of his own party. The healthcare law which attempts to serve two masters—social welfare and corporate profits—serves both poorly. Meaningful financial reform has been effectively blocked; even the modest reform that was passed is relatively toothless. Even should Obama win reelection against Wall Street's candidate (a prospect that given the anemic economic recovery and the corporate money flowing into the 2012 election tenuous), the corporate exploitation of the environment, consumers, and workers will continue unabated. The elite will again be bailed out after the next financial collapse; the military-industrial complex will strengthen; the inequality of income and wealth will continue to rise; the social safety net will continue to fray; the environment will continue to suffer. Change will certainly come, but only after serious upheaval and revolution.

I end as I began, with Weber: "This order is now bound to the technical and economic conditions of machine production which to-day determine the lives of all individuals who are born into this mechanism, not only those directly concerned with economic acquisition, with irresistible force. *Perhaps it will so determine them until the last ton of fossilized coal is burnt.* In Baxter's view the care for external goods should only lie on the shoulders of the 'saint like a light cloak, which can be thrown aside at any moment.' But fate decreed that the cloak should become an iron cage" (1904/1930, 181; emphasis added). Such an iron cage will be difficult to escape or dismantle.

References:

American Civil Liberties Union. 2010. Surveillance Under the U.S. Patriot Act. http://www.aclu.org/national-security/surveillance-under-usa-patriot-act

Barney, Gerald O. (study director). 1980. The Global 2000 Report to the President, 3 vols. Washington D.C.: U.S. Government Printing Office.

Berry, Wendell. 1977. The Unsettling of America. New York: Avon Books.

Burnham, David. 1980. The Rise of the Computer State. New York: Vintage Books.

Cohen, Mark. 1977. The Food Crisis in Prehistory: Over Population and the Origins of Agriculture. New Haven: Yale University Press.

Cole, M.S.D. 1973. Models of Doom. New York: Universe

Diamond, Jared. 2005. *Collapse: How Societies Choose to Fail or Succeed.* New York: Penguin Group.

Domhoff, G. William. 1967. Who Rules America? New Jersey: Prentice-Hall, Inc.

Dye, Thomas R. 1983. Who's Running America? The Reagan Years. Third Edition. New Jersey: Prentice-Hall, Inc.

Dye, Thomas R. 2002. Who's Running America? The Bush Restoration. Seventh Edition. New Jersey: Prentice-Hall, Inc.

Edgerton, Les. 2012. "Hiring the write employee." Dental Economics. http://www.dentaleconomics.com/index/display/article-display/123070/articles/dental-economics/volume-86/issue-9/features/hiring-the-write-employee.html

Elwell, Frank W. 1991. *The Evolution of the Future.* West Port: Praeger.

Elwell, Frank W. 1999. *Industrializing America: Understanding Contemporary Society Through Classical Sociological Analysis.* West Port: Praeger.

Elwell, Frank W. 2001. *A Commentary on Malthus' 1798 Essay on the Principle of Population as Social Theory*. Lewiston: Mellen Press.

Elwell, Frank W. 2006. *Macrosociology: Four Modern Theorists*. Boulder: Paradigm Publishers.

Elwell, Frank W. 2009. *Macrosociology: The Study of Sociocultural Systems*. Lewiston: Mellen Press.

Elwell, Frank W. 2009b. "Harry Braverman and the working class." In *Bureaucratic Culture and Escalating World Problems: Advancing the Sociological Imagination.* (D. Knottnerus and B. Phillips, eds.) 85-98. Boulder: Paradigm Publishers.

Elwell, Frank W. 2013 *Sociocultural Systems: Principles of Structure and Change.* Canada: Athabasca University Press.

Freund, Julien. 1969. The Sociology of Max Weber. New York: Vintage Books.

Harrington, Michael. 1976. The Twilight of Capitalism. New York: Touchstone.

Harris, Marvin. 1974. Cows, Pigs, Wars and Witches: The Riddles of Culture. New York: Vintage Books.

Harris, Marvin. 1977. Cannibals and Kings: The Origins of Cultures. New York: Vintage Books.

Harris, Marvin. 1979. Cultural Materialism: The Struggle for a Science of Culture. New York: Random House.

Harris, Marvin. 1981. America Now: The Anthropology of a Changing Culture. New York: Simon & Schuster.

Heilbroner, Robert. 1980. An Inquiry Into the Human Prospect. New York: W. W. Norton & Co.

Howard, Robert. 1985. Brave New Workplace. Virginia: R. R. Donnelley & Sons Co.

Huxley, Aldous. 1959. Brave New World Revisited. New York: Harper & Row.

International Monetary Fund (IMF). 2012. Debt of Emerging and Developing Economies. http://www.imf.org/external/pubs/ft/weo/2012/01/weodata/weoselagr.aspx#a200

Kumar, Krishan. 1978. Prophecy and Progress. New York: Penguin Books.

Lasch, Christopher. 1979. The Culture of Narcissism. New York: Warner Books.

Meadows, Donella, et al. 1972. The Limits of Growth. New York: New American Library.

Meadows, Dennis, and Donella Meadows (eds.). 1973. Toward Global Equilibrium: Collected Papers. Massachusetts: Wright-Allen Press, Inc.

Meadows, Dennis, et al. 1974. Dynamics of Growth in a Finite World. Massachusetts: Wright-Allen Press, Inc.

Menosky, Joseph A. 1984. "Computer Worship," Science 84, May, 40-46.

Michels, Robert 1915/1962. Political Parties: A Sociological Study of the Oligarchical Tendencies of Modern Democracies. New York: The MacMillan Company.

Mills, C. Wright. 1951. White Collar: The American Middle Classes. New York: Oxford University Press.

Mills, C. Wright. 1956. The Power Elite. New York: Oxford University Press.

Mills, C. Wright. 1959. The Sociological Imagination. New York: Oxford University Press.

Naisbitt, John. 1982. Megatrends. New York: Warner Books, Inc.

Parenti, Michael. 1978. Power and the Powerless. New York: St. Martin's Press.

Rifkin, Jeremy. 1980. Entropy: A New World View. New York: Bantam Books.

Sharp, Gwen. 2011. "Concentration in U.S. agriculture." http://thesocietypages.org/ socimages/ 2011/07/23/concentration-in-u-s-agriculture/

Taibbi, M. 2012. "How Wall Street killed financial reform." Rolling Stone, May.

http://www.rollingstone.com/politics/news/how-wall-street-killed-financial-reform-20120510

Toeffler, Alvin. 1981. The Third Wave. New York: Bantam Books.

Weber, Max. 1904/1930. *The Protestant Ethic and the Spirit of Capitalism.* (T. Parsons, Trans.) New York: The Citadel Press.

Weber, Max. 1921/1968. *Economy and Society.* (G. Roth, C. Wittich, Eds., G. Roth, & C. Wittich, Trans.) New York: Bedminster Press.

Winner, Langdon. 1984. "Mythinformation in the high-tech era." IEEE Spectrum, June, 90-96.

World Bank. 2012. "Population Growth Rate." http://www.worldbank.org/depweb/english/modules/social/pgr/

World Health Organization (WHO) 2012. "The Urban Environment."

http://www.who.int/heli/risks/urban/urbanenv/en/

United Nations Population Fund. 2007. "Unleashing the Potential of Urban Growth."

http://www.unfpa.org/swp/2007/english/introduction.html